About the Author

Shemal Samuelson, a Kurdish woman, was born and liberally raised in the Iranian part of Kurdistan. Shemal came to Norway as a political refugee in the '80s. She moved to Sweden through marriage in the '90s. She graduated as a medical doctor from the University of Uppsala and qualified as an ENT consultant. Shemal has during her eventful life always been actively engaged in women's rights, gender equality, and humanism. This book is her second. The first book is her autobiography released in Swedish in 2021.

The Prison Guard

Shemal Samuelson

The Prison Guard

Olympia Publishers
London

www.olympiapublishers.com
OLYMPIA PAPERBACK EDITION

Copyright © Shemal Samuelson 2023

The right of Shemal Samuelson to be identified as author of this work has been asserted in accordance with sections 77 and 78 of the Copyright, Designs and Patents Act 1988.

All Rights Reserved

No reproduction, copy or transmission of this publication may be made without written permission.
No paragraph of this publication may be reproduced, copied or transmitted save with the written permission of the publisher, or in accordance with the provisions of the Copyright Act 1956 (as amended).

Any person who commits any unauthorised act in relation to this publication may be liable to criminal prosecution and civil claims for damage.

A CIP catalogue record for this title is available from the British Library.

ISBN: 978-1-80439-651-3

This is a work of creative nonfiction. The events are portrayed to the best of the author's memory. While all the stories in this book are true, some names and identifying details have been changed to protect the privacy of the people involved.

First Published in 2023

Olympia Publishers
Tallis House
2 Tallis Street
London
EC4Y 0AB

Printed in Great Britain

Dedication

Dedicated to Surreya, Mahnaz and all the nameless women who were exploited and victimized.

Acknowledgements

Thanks! – I would like to convey to my husband Per, who with his support and positive enthusiasm has given me the opportunity to complete this book. Thanks to Anders Ehrnborn who professionally translated the manuscript from Swedish to English. Thanks also to Olympia publishing house for support and publishing this book.

Preface

My father became a political prisoner in Iran in 1981. He and we all lived under the threat that he would be executed. During my quarterly visits to the prison in Orumiyeh, I got to know some people, especially women. Their fates were etched in me and by recounting their history I want to honor and preserve their memory.

The story describes women's vulnerability. How they are unconscionably exploited by autocratic people. In this case, how the mullahs in Iran and their subordinates in the name of the regime and religion behave towards the defenseless. Where one is the "law" and without any human emotions, the most terrible abuses are carried out.

I tell you about the few that I learned about, but believe me, there were many more who were sexually abused, tortured, and then murdered. They died alone in silence, without anyone daring to talk about them, and without their families being allowed to see their bodies or bury them!

Vasterås, Spring 2022
Shemal Samuelson

Hundreds of people sat in the hot summer day outside the large prison in Orumiyeh, a Kurdish city in northwestern Iran on Lake Urmia. It was over forty degrees Celsius and there were no trees providing shade. There were no benches to sit on. People sat on the ground. Many stood or walked back and forth in their turmoil. They were relatives of the political prisoners who were incarcerated in prison. It was visiting day, and everyone was waiting for the prison guards to let them in so they could visit or talk on the phone with their incarcerated relatives. Worry, sorrow and fear could be seen in every face of those waiting. The prison was a large building hidden from all sides behind soaring concrete walls. At the top of their watchtowers in the north, south, west and east corners, armed guards stood ready to fire. The prison is located just outside the city towards the lake.

I was there with my uncle waiting to meet my father, who had been missing for four months after he had been arrested at home. We had recently learned that he was inside the prison. I was nervous, very emotionally charged, and walked back and forth along the prison wall. I saw old men and women who were sad and crying.

I also saw younger women, many were dressed in black, and sad, but a few had put on makeup as if they were going to a party. I didn't understand them. Everyone spoke Kurdish. Only Kurdish political prisoners were imprisoned here.

I walked around among the people waiting. An old woman held her hand to me. She had a piece of paper rolled in her hand. She wanted me to help her read the note to the prison guard when they opened the gates. On the paper was a name and the age of her son. I promised to do so and helped her move closer to the door, where my uncle and I stood waiting. She had trouble walking and had a half-bent back. A deformed, wrinkled old mother, filled with sadness and fear for her son's life.

My uncle was a little angry with me for not being able to calm down. He wanted me to stand still near him. But I couldn't do it, I was restless and nervous that I wouldn't be able to see my father. That they would instead inform us that he had been executed during the night. I felt my pulse increase, and my heartbeat in the pit of my throat, I was in a cold sweat in waves and nauseous. I asked the old lady to remain close to my uncle and walked around again to distract my thoughts, to avoid having to look at the large prison door waiting for it to open.

In the crowd, I saw a young woman who looked different from the others. She was dressed in a long black coat and wore a colorful shawl over her hair. Her face was heavily made up with blue eyeshadow and bright red lips. She was bothered by me looking at her and said:

"What are you gloating about? What are you thinking about?"

I stepped closer to her, greeted her politely, and said:

"I am here to know if my father Ahmad Kamrani is alive, if I can meet him and hear his voice. I don't feel well and I'm very nervous. Who are you waiting to meet?"

She looked at me kindly and said:

"Hey, I know who you are! I have my husband in there. He is twenty-two years old. We've only been married for three months. I want to see him and tell him that I will wait for him, even if it will be many years before he can be free."

"Do you know if he's alive? Have you been seeing him since he was imprisoned?"

She sighed and replied, "Yes, but it has cost me a lot!"

"Do you mean money and gold?"

"No, my body and my soul!"

"Oops, what do you mean? How?"

"I can't talk about it now, but if you want, we can meet later."

"What city are you from?"

"Same city as you, I'm from Khaneh."

She took a paper and pen out of her bag, wrote her name, address and phone number, and handed it to me.

"Do you have anyone with you?"

"No, I'm not allowed to have anyone with me!"

"Why?"

"I'll tell you then." She smiled a pale smile that was full of sadness.

We heard the exclamation in Farsi from the loudspeaker urging all the relatives to back away from the door and wall:

"They will shout the names of the prisoners who have visiting rights today. The prison guards will lead the relatives in. Everyone must show ID card, shenasnameh."

People backed off as they pushed each other to take their place further in line. Many of these people understood neither Farsi nor Azeri, which were the only languages the information was given in.

We stood there listening, waiting to hear my dad's name called. I felt like I was shaking and had a dry mouth and saw that the young woman I had been talking to was being picked up by a prison guard. She followed him inside and disappeared behind the prison door.

At last, they called out my father's name.

"Ahmad Kamrani, relatives of Ahmad Kamrani."

My uncle took quick steps towards the open door, and I followed him. At the door we met the prison guard who led us inside. He complained that my hijab was not comprehensive. My coat was knee length, and it should have been ankle length. I was told that I couldn't let a single hair be seen. I pulled my shawl to my forehead. He approved it a little angrily and led us in. We first entered a long and obscure corridor.

Then we passed labyrinthine dark corridors until we arrived at another slightly lighter corridor with tens of windows in a row along the wall. The windows were separated from each other by cement walls. The windows were of double thick glass and insulated so that you could not hear each other through the glass. There was an old gray phone on each side as a connection.

We waited at one of these glass walls and then I saw my dad coming.

He couldn't walk. Two prison guards held him under his arms and pulled him towards us on the inside. Dad was so pale. His mouth was slanted. Half his face and one eye were blue marbled. His one ear was bandaged. He stood there looking at us through the glass wall. I burst into a crying attack. My uncle was also crying and shook. Dad looked at us and his tears flowed.

His eyes were blank. His body was worn out. My dad, who was a big and powerful man, was now almost half his size. He had lost many pounds in weight. I picked up the phone. Dad lifted his handset on the other side. His eyes spoke to me and said: "Don't show weakness, talk!"

"Hey, Dad, how are you? I've missed you so much."

He replied in a weak voice that was full of sadness and anger, "I'm freezing, I need warm clothes that can keep my body warm. I sleep on a bare cement floor."

"I'll fix it, Dad. I will bring you warm clothes on my next

visit."

My uncle took the phone from me so that he too could talk to his brother before the time was up. He talked to him in codes, but I knew what the words meant.

"Ahmad, don't worry. I have taken care of all the fruits on the farm. The trees will soon give ripe fruit and I will bring fruit to you when I come to visit the next time!"

The visiting time, which was only five minutes, quickly ran out. The prison guards pulled on Dad's arms and carried him away. His last glance at me said a lot. Trying to avoid showing my weakness, I sent kisses to Dad with my hand. He disappeared from our sight. We were immediately led by the guard towards the exit.

I remembered that I was going to help the old lady out there and ran off towards the exit but was immediately stopped by a guard.

"Hello! You are not allowed to run here. Where are you going?"

"An elderly lady, the mother of a prisoner here, can't talk Farsi, she needs help. I promised I would help her."

"What's her name?"

"Don't know, she showed her son's name which was written on a piece of paper."

"What's his name?"

"Faroq Rezaei."

"Calm down. She's been inside and met her son. She's already gone home!"

I doubted what he said. She couldn't have been inside already and met her son!

"Thanks, then I know. I'm going home."

He showed me the way to the exit. I went out and still saw

lots of people waiting. I walked towards them, looking for the old lady. A man recognized me.

"Who are you looking for? How was your father?"

"Yes, thank you, it was okay with my father," I replied gently. I'm looking for the old lady who was going to meet her son. She didn't know Farsi and needed help."

He shook his head and answered.

"Go home, my daughter. She was told her son was executed yesterday. She passed out. A fellow human took her in his car to the hospital."

"Huh… are you serious? That lady who had a bent back and was thin and worn?"

"Yes, my daughter, she is from my city of Nagadeh. I interpreted for her when the prison guard gave the message. I think she's already dead. She had a heart attack right away when I translated what the prison guard read from the paper he had brought with him. He wanted her to come back with a male relative and fifty thousand tuman to pay for the ammunition they had shot her son with. Then they would be able to get his body back to bury."

"My God." I burst into tears again. I felt immense guilt that I forgot her, and I wasn't there to support her when she got the heartbreaking news. My uncle came and held me when I was shaking and crying. The man told him what had happened. My uncle pulled me towards the car that was parked some distance away.

***

We came back home after three hours of driving from Orumiyeh. We sat in silence in the car all the way home. We were shocked and saddened to have seen my dad this way. My uncle left me at the door. He drove to his home in Shno which was forty kilometers from Khaneh.

After my father was arrested, the Islamic regime seized our big house and everything that was in my father's possession. Our family had to move to a smaller accommodation with a bonus grandfather. There was only one room, which we all ate and slept in, a smaller bathroom and a small kitchen corner. Stepmother, me and my five younger siblings slept in the same room on mattresses. My sister Nasrin was four years younger than me, and my brothers were ten, eight, six and two years old.

My grandma died, a month after Dad was arrested, in a bus on the way to Orumiyeh to look for Dad. Her death was another hard blow to me after Dad's arrest.

I had learned that my stepmother was pregnant and expecting her sixth child. She was often out of town with my uncle or her brother to find contacts among the regime's principals who could be influenced to alleviate my father's judgment. When she got home, she was so tired that she couldn't bear anything but eat and sleep. As the eldest daughter in the family, all responsibility for the home and my younger siblings rested on me. I was barely seventeen years old and lived like a poor mother with several young children. All our money and possessions were confiscated by the regime. By sewing and embroidering for others, I made some money for our everyday lives.

It was three o'clock in the afternoon when I got home from Orumiyeh and as soon as I stepped in, Stepmother said.

"You have to shop and cook for the evening for everyone. I don't feel well and need to rest."

"Okay, I'll go shopping. I'll also have to buy yarn to knit a sweater and pants for Dad for the next visit."

"Why knitting? He's got prison clothes, doesn't he?"

"He said he's freezing. He sleeps on cement floors. I'm going to knit clothes out of wool yarn that can keep him warm."

"Okay, here, you get three hundred tuman."

I bought fifteen skeins of wool yarn in gray and black colors from which I would knit a sweater and some trousers. I also bought some long, slightly thicker wooden sticks to be able to knit thickly.

It was ten o'clock in the evening. We had eaten and I had time to clean the kitchen. My stepmother and the children fell asleep before the electricity was shut down by the regime every night, as usual. I lit an oil lamp and began to knit under the sparse lighting.

***

At five o'clock in the morning I had knitted half the sweater for Dad. Tired, I turned off the light and lay down next to my youngest brother to sleep for a few hours.

The next morning, I wanted to call Surreya, the newlywed woman from the prison yard.

We didn't have a phone at our house, but I was going home to an uncle, who had a home phone. I was so curious about what she meant by it costing her body and soul. I took my youngest brother Shoresh with me and walked home to my uncle. Shoresh was so attached to me and became insecure when he didn't see me.

At my uncle's house, I asked my cousin to look after Shoresh and guard so that no one would hear while I was talking on the phone. I didn't want to tell anyone about Surreya. She smiled and said:

"Are you calling that guy you're in love with?"

"Yes... Please don't let anyone hear. Call out to me if your mother is coming."

"Yes, I'll do it. Go in and hurry up."

I went inside and took out the note with Surreya's number on it, which was hidden in my bra. With my heart pounding, I dialed the number.

"Hey, it's Surreya! Who is it?"

"Hi, Surreya, I'm Shemal Kamrani. We met yesterday at the prison in Orumiyeh."

"Yes... Hey how did it go yesterday? Hope your father is well!"

"Yes... like that, but he's alive and I'm happy about that."

"I see."

"Can we meet? I want to hear about what you told me yesterday. I've been thinking about you and what you said."

"Yes... I can't talk about it on the phone. But we can meet at my house or at your house, if you want."

"I haven't told my stepmother about you and not anyone else either. Who do you live with? I can come to you."

"Okay, I live with my parents in-law. The mother-in-law is kind and does not ask who I am dating or why. The father-in-law works in his shop and comes home late at night."

"Then I'd rather come to your house. But I must have my two-year-old brother with me, is that okay?"

"Okay, you can come tomorrow afternoon. You don't have to call, come when you can."

"Thanks, see you tomorrow!"

I came out of the room and met my cousin who had a smile on her face.

"Date tomorrow, do you need a babysitter for Shoresh?"
"No, I'll bring him."

She had been eavesdropping but didn't understand who I'd been talking to.

Now that everyone had gone back to bed, I sat and knitted and thought about Surreya. "What will she tell me tomorrow? Is it any good? Or tragic?"

But I wanted to know that anyway. I felt sympathy for her who was a young newlywed, beautiful woman and her husband who was in prison. Maybe I could support her somehow?

The first wool sweater for Dad was finished so I started knitting his pants. It was a very thick, nice sweater in black color with a gray striped pattern. The thought of these clothes keeping his body warm made me happy, so I wanted to sit and knit all night. During the day, I didn't have time because the housework, siblings and needlework took all my time.

***

It was three o'clock in the afternoon the next day and I had said I would visit a friend and take my little brother Shoresh along. Stepmother had gone to Nagadeh for a doctor's visit. My sister Nasrin promised not to gossip to Mom if I brought home some candy or anything else good. She would take care of our three younger brothers.

I carried Shoresh in my arms and walked towards Surreya's home which was two blocks away.

"Hey welcome, come in step on."
"Thanks."

We went in after her, passed through a yard with several fruit trees and a small vegetable garden. We came to a house with a large terrace in front. I saw that she had set the table and planned for us to sit on the terrace. Shoresh was given a small plastic ball to play with. He was delighted and ran away for the ball.

We each sat on a pillow on a handmade rug on the terrace.

"Is your mother-in-law home?"

"No, she's with her sister who lives across the street. She goes there almost every day."

"How good that she has someone to talk to and share her grief."

"Yes, they are very sad that my husband, who is their youngest son, is in prison. And their two older sons are peshmerga of Komala, which is the political left wing of the peshmerga."

"Does Komala also call its armed force peshmerga?"

"Yes, you know that peshmerga means 'he who fights for freedom'. All Kurds who fight actively for freedom, regardless of party-political opinion, are called peshmerga."

"Was your husband also peshmerga?"

"Not directly, but a supporter of Komala."

"When did you get married? Was it love or…"

She interrupted me.

"Yes, it was a genuine love. We had a love affair for three years. I had to run away from home in order to marry him. My parents planned to marry me off to another man."

"Oh, run away from home! To whom and where?"

"I came to my in-laws' house one late afternoon and said I refused to leave. Sirwan and I love each other, and you have to help us so we can get married. They were very kind and accepted me as their own child. A week later, a mullah wed me and Sirwan as husband and wife. There was a small family celebration here at home. We were so happy and so happily married. But this stupid Islamic regime came and sabotaged everything for us and for everyone."

"How sad. Hope he comes out soon. Do you know about my dad?"

"Yes, of course everyone knows who Agayeh Kamrani is. All of us in the family cried when we heard that he too had been arrested. How is he doing?"

"He's under threat of being executed. He has been tortured. I saw that on him the other day when we visited him. We are working on everything we can to save him from execution."

Surreya cried and hugged me.

"We all pray for him. He is a fine man. I hope God will help him."

"Thanks, Surreya, now I'd love to hear what you couldn't tell me about on the phone."

"Listen, I haven't told anyone this so far. It's dangerous both for me and for my husband sitting inside. But I don't know why I trust you. I need to talk about it with someone. I have cried in my loneliness and not been able to tell anyone about my grief and vulnerability. I feel like I can do it for you. Do you promise you'll never tell anyone?"

"Yes, I promise never to tell anyone. I swear on my dad's life which is the most important thing to me."

"I want us not to show openly that we are friends. It can become dangerous for you."

"Why dangerous?"

"You'll understand when I've told you everything I've been exposed to."

"I'm listening. I want you to feel safe with me."

"I do, you're just like an adult wise person even though you're younger than me."

"How do you know I'm younger?"

"I know about you; you were in the same class as my brother. He used to talk about you sometimes!"

"Aha, then I know why."

"Listen, if my mother-in-law comes in, then we'll change the topic of conversation, okay?"

"Yes, absolutely. I'm listening."

"When they arrested Sirwan out on the town, we weren't even told where he was or who had arrested him. For a whole month, my in-laws were looking for their son. Finally, via a djash, Kurds who work for and cooperate with the regime, they got in touch with a responsible mullah in Orumiyeh to whom they paid lots of money. He found my husband among the political prisoners in the prison there. The first time we got to visit him, I was with my in-laws, but they just let me and the mother-in-law go in and meet Sirwan behind the glass wall. My mother-in-law fainted when she saw her son in such poor condition as he was. He was skinny and pale as a corpse. He had lots of wounds on his face and his eyes were bruised and swollen. You could see how they had tortured him. I cried behind the phone when Sirwan said this was the last time I could see and talk to him. He had been told that they would execute him if he did not cooperate with them. He would rather die than cooperate with the regime, he said. When I turned around after our brief conversation ended, I saw Reza, the prison guard, who had let me and the mother-in-law in. He stood there waiting for me!

"He said he had carried my mother-in-law, who fell passed out, to a room while I was talking to Sirwan. He wanted me to accompany him to the room where the mother-in-law lay. I followed and he took me to a room that was dark with only a low bed and some other gadgets. Neither my mother-in-law nor any other people were there. I was frightened, thinking that I too would be imprisoned, but he said this to me, 'Do you want to save your husband from execution?'

"'Yes please, I want to do everything to save him. Please help me. We've only been married for three months. We love each other so much.'

"He hugged me and pressed me against his chest. I was so sad and scared that it felt good that he showed empathy. But he began to push me more and more against him, caressing my breasts and butt. I got scared and pulled away. He became serious in his voice.

"'If you deny me, I'll make sure he gets executed tonight. But if you become my mistress and obey me in everything I ask, I can make sure he lives in prison, and you can see him often. You don't tell anyone, not even your in-laws. If you deviate once, it will cost you your husband's life, just so you know.'

"'But please, I'm a married woman! It is haram, religiously forbidden, to sleep with another man,' I whispered.

"'Oh, we don't care about haram! Everyone does it, even the mullahs themselves have a lot of women.'

"'But I love my husband, I can't sleep with anyone else.'

"'If you love him, you should save his life.'

"'How do I know you have the influence to save him from execution?'

"'I have a close relationship with Ayatollah Khalkhali. I can get him to change your husband's verdict. You're going to see it. But only if you make me happy and satisfied all the time, I request it.'

"'Okay, I'll do it,' I cried. 'But where is my mother-in-law?'

"'She's in a room near the entrance. A nurse and your father-in-law are with her. She is awake and has been given a drip and medicine by the nurse.'

"'But they're going to wonder where I am now.'

"'No, they think you're out waiting for them. I've asked the nurse not to let them out before I tell them to.'

"'Okay, I'll do as you please.'"

Surreya began to cry, she wiped away her tears and looked towards the outside door. She went in and fetched us a tray of tea, small cakes and some fruit on the terrace.

"Do you want to hear more or is it hard?" she asked.

"It's horrible but I want to hear everything."

"He raped me there in my room like a hungry wild animal. I just closed my eyes and thought about Sirwan's life. When he was done, he followed me to the exit and said, 'I'll call you home and say Sirwan has visiting hours. Then I want you to come alone.'

"'You can't. My in-laws don't send me off to Orumiyeh alone.'

"'I'm going to fix a letter from us to them. That they can only meet their son once a month, but you, as his wife, can see him more often. They cannot deny our order. I want you every time you come here to be well dressed, showered, shaved legs and lower abdomen and made up like a bride to me.'

"'But it can expose us. My in-laws will question that.'

"'I can make sure you spend the night with your husband sometimes. Then you can say that you are doing it to make him happy.'

"'Okay, as you decide. But promise you'll stop Sirwan's execution sentence.'

"'I promise, I can help Sirwan, so he calls home next week and tells them himself.'

"I was so happy and hopeful about saving Sirwan's life that

I forgot the pain of the rape.

"Sirwan called home just five days later and told them he had received an amnesty on his death sentence. He would be in prison for ten years instead. I was overjoyed to hear that. My in-laws gave lots of alms to the poor in gratitude to God for saving their son's life.

"I was proud of myself because I was the one who really saved their son's life.

"Reza, the prison guard, established a very close relationship with my in-laws and also with Sirwan in there. They all loved him and trusted his word one hundred percent.

***

"He persuaded them to send me alone to Orumiyeh for arranging overnight visits for me and my husband. My father-in-law would then go on the trip to prison, leave me there and go home by himself. He came back again the next day to pick me up from prison. The mother-in-law and father-in-law were pleased and happy that Sirwan and I could meet and be together. My father-in-law bought expensive gifts for Reza every time because he was so helpful to us!

"My mother-in-law thought it was good that I dressed nicely and put on makeup when I was going to visit Sirwan. Then he would be happy and have the energy to wait another ten years in prison! She made sure I had the money to buy nice new clothes, perfume and everything I needed!

"The first few times Reza used to take me to a room in the prison and for a few hours he would rape me several times. He used to have so much fruit, drinks, cakes and food in the room that it was enough even for me and Sirwan overnight. There was a bed, a chair, some plates and cutlery, glasses and teacups in the room. But no windows and the door was a heavy iron door that could be locked from the inside.

"He said it was his own room where he could rest and sleep between shifts. No one else had a key to the room. Once he was satisfied, he left me alone in the room until the evening when he brought Sirwan to me and locked the door from outside. I fixed up the room so when Sirwan arrived he thought I had just arrived."

"Wasn't it hard to have intimate contact with Sirwan on the same day?"

"Well, I usually had a lot of pain in my lower abdomen because Reza was very hard and aggressive when he was excited. I had a hard time relaxing when Sirwan wanted to have sex. I was tense the whole time, but Sirwan was so soft and loving that I could cope with the pains, both the bodily and the ones in my soul."

"Didn't Sirwan ask why his parents didn't come to visit?"

"Reza had tricked him that according to Islamic rules, they had allowed all the men in the prison to see their wives more often to have sex. But for parents, one visits every two months was enough!"

"How long has this been going on?"

"One year, it's been a year since Sirwan was imprisoned."

"Is Reza still interested in you? Is he kind to you?"

"He beat and threatened me two months ago when I told him I hadn't had my period and maybe I was pregnant. He ordered me to have an abortion. When I said that maybe it was my husband, I had gotten pregnant with and I wanted to keep the baby, he became very aggressive and kicked me in the back for me to have a miscarriage. He threatened me that until next time, if I didn't have an abortion and didn't put in an IUD, he would make sure Sirwan was tortured. I was terrified and went to a doctor who gave me many tablets to take over three days. Then I had a hemorrhage and very painful menstrual cramps. Two weeks later, the same doctor put an IUD in me."

"And then what? What happened after that?"

"I've been there twice a month and each time Reza has raped me several times and then left me with Sirwan at night."

"Hasn't Sirwan noticed something?"

"He's sometimes said I'm cold to him, that I'm not the same. But he says he understands why."

"Why? Why according to him?"

"He thinks it's because I know he's a prisoner, that we don't have a normal life together, that I'm sad and not feeling well. I have confirmed that it is true what he says. He wants me to get pregnant and have a child that can make his parents happy. But I've said I don't want our child to see his dad in jail."

"How are you going to continue this for ten years?"

"Do I have a choice? Reza will make sure Sirwan is tortured and executed if I don't agree to his orders!"

"Do you think there are more women who are exposed to this? Who are victims like you?"

"Yes, I know of three other women that Reza has told me about."

"What... does he know about the vulnerability of other women?"

"He's the boss of all the prison guards. He knows everything about everyone. He told me that a thirteen-year-old girl was raped by Ayatollah Khalkhali for him to change her father's execution sentence. So, beware lest they catch their eyes on you! You with your green eyes and fair skin could be the dream of these dirty men!"

"But how the hell can a thirteen-year-old girl cope with an old man who is older than her father? Is the girl alive?"

"Yes, she now lives in a house as Khalkhali's secret wife. He has performed the temporary religious marriage according to the law of the Shiites! Reza said Khalkhali doesn't want to let her go just yet!"

"What happened to the girl's father?"

"He was given a prison sentence instead of execution and is in prison."

"What else do you know about this girl or other women who have been affected? How can I get in touch with her?"

Surreya smiled at me and said:

"Beware, don't play with fire. She is a luxury living prisoner of Ayatollah Khalkhali. No one can access her as long as he wants her. Want to play journalist... Hehe!"

"But please, can't you try to get a clue via Reza? I promise to be very careful. I don't take any risks. But I want to know more about her. What her name is and where she lives."

Surreya interrupted me and continued, "Another married woman like me, where her husband was doomed to be executed, has saved her husband by becoming a mistress and spy for them."

"Whoa, who is she? I must watch out for her."

"Her name is Halima and she's from Nagadeh. She has blue eyes. She is between thirty and forty years old, beautiful and talkative."

"Thanks, I'll be careful if I meet her. What can I do to help you, Surreya?"

"You can't do more than listen to me and keep my secret right now."

"How long do you think you're going to be able to do this?

What do you feel about Reza?"

"I don't know how long I'm going to be able to do this, but as long as Sirwan lives, I'll do it. I hate Reza and I dream many times that I am strangling him with my own hands. I've sometimes thought about taking a knife with me and murdering him, but I know it will cost Sirwan his life. I hate him and even myself when I pretend to enjoy having sex with Reza. But I live on the hope that Sirwan can be free one day.

"Then I will tell him everything. Then I and Sirwan will become peshmerga and kill Reza and everyone like him."

"I hope, Surreya, that the beautiful day will come when Sirwan, my father and all political prisoners will be free. Oops, it's already five o'clock and I have to go home. But can we see each other sometimes? We don't have a phone at home right now."

"I know where you live, I can send a note or come by somehow."

"Okay, let me know when you need to talk. I promise I'm there for you and I'll keep it a secret."

"Thanks, I'm safe with you, it feels good. Goodbye my friend."

"Goodbye, Surreya."

I took my little brother and walked away quickly. I had to make it home before my stepmother would be suspicious.

***

It had been two weeks since I started knitting clothes for my dad. I had knitted two rounds of lined wool sweater and trousers. The next week, Stepmother and Uncle would go to Orumiyeh and visit Dad. Then they would take the clothes with them. I wrote a simple letter to my father and put it between the clothes. It had to be written so that those responsible in prison did not throw away the letter. I had to pretend that I was a Muslim and respected Islamic rule. I wrote like this:

Bismillahe rahamnarahim; In the name of the kind and bestowing God!

My beloved and missed Dad! I have knitted these clothes with my love and my thoughts for you. I know that our good God will help you and we pray for you all the time. I miss you infinitely. Your Daughter/Shemal.

My stepmother was skeptical to bring the letter, but I asked her so much that in the end she accepted it. They left early in the morning, and I had to take care of the home and my siblings.

I've been thinking about everything Surreya told me the other day. I may not be able to feel her pain for real like she does, but I'm sad about her suffering and I'm feeling more and more hate for the Islamic regime and all the things they're doing to people.

I have not been able to let go of my thoughts of the thirteen-year-old girl who is a prisoner of a sadistic old mullah like Khalkhali. I've seen her in my dreams where her face is bloody and running barefoot with torn clothes. Every time I wake up from these dreams, I promise myself I'll have to find her. I have to help her.

I've even thought about different scenarios, that once I know where she is, how I'm going to be able to go to her house to talk to her. I can pretend to be a beggar or a salesman selling handmade things.

***

I had to wash all our bedding by hand, as we didn't have a washing machine. I boiled water over the gas stove and washed the white sheets in a metal tub, which we call tasht. A hard job, but I have to do it. Nasrin, my little sister, looked after our four little brothers. Bonus Grandma had said we could all eat at their place on this day, since our mom wasn't at home, and I had laundry day.

Behind Grandpa's large house, which was high up on the hillside and high above the street, ran a rushing stream. Everyone in the area came there when they wanted to wash clothes or wash large pots.

I first carried my laundry in a basket and then the hot water in a bucket up to the creek behind the house. There I sat down on a rock and began to wash. There were a few more women sitting and washing clothes on the other side of the creek.

Some young girls on my side were doing the dishes. It was sociable and actually a little bit of fun. You always had company when you washed there.

I had made it halfway through my washing when I saw my second youngest brother, Wafa, come and show me to a young lady wearing a black chador, a full-face cape. She approached and I saw that it was Surreya.

"Hey, Surreya, how nice that you showed up. Who told you I'm here?"

"Hey, Shemal gyan, I came up the stairs and saw your little brother. I saw from his appearance that he must be your brother, he looks just like you. I asked for you and he came along and showed me that you were here. No one else was there. How are you? Should I help you with the laundry?"

"Nope. Sit on this rock and talk to me instead."

Surreya took her chador, folded it, and put it on the stone as a pillow to sit on.

"I was in Orumiyeh two days ago to meet Sirwan."

"Aha, how did it go? Was there an overnight stay again?"

"Yes, like all the times, Reza raped me first, then I got to meet Sirwan. You know, my suffering always goes hand in hand with my hope when I visit Sirwan. But I may have an answer to something you'd love to know. I managed to get the name of the thirteen-year-old girl who is the secret wife of Khalkhali!"

"Oh, how good, how? Tell me!"

"I tested Reza a little bit and asked if he would like me as his own wife, like the girl with Khalkhali. He said he couldn't support two wives at the same time. He has a wife and three children. I then asked how and where Khalkhali had taken that girl Laleh? Then he spontaneously said, 'Her name is Mahnaz, not Laleh. Khalkhali has rented an apartment in the city in one of the remote areas. She lives anonymously and under a different name there. An elderly lady who is Khalkhali's family and a widow lives with her in the house all the time and suits her. She can never go out by herself. They don't have a home phone either.'"

"Did you find out on which street she lives?"

"Yes, I asked Reza, if sometimes we'd like to sleep a whole night together, couldn't we stay with them then?

"Without thinking, he answered directly, 'They live three houses away from my family. I can't, but I might find another place.'

"I pretended I knew where he lived and asked him, 'But you and your family live centrally in Orumiyeh don't you? Wasn't it on Imam-street?'

"'No, you've got the wrong address. I live in Shekhtappa, right where the newly built apartments are. The high apartments.

I live in number two and Ayatollah Khalkhali with his young wife in number seven.'

"'Aha, that's right. I'd forgotten you told me.'

"'Good, you're so smart and brave.'

"I was like a real actor to him that night. I think he was influenced by something. He was incredibly cheerful and in a good mood. He showed no resistance to my questions as he otherwise used to."

"He might have smoked some tiriac, opium!"

"Yes, I think so. He smelled strange, and his eyes were red and strange. But now we know where she lives and what her name is. But what do you intend to do? Maybe I can help if I know what you want?"

"I've actually thought a lot about her and how to help her. But we must first know how she feels. She might be happy with her life as it is. How can we get in contact with her? That's the most important step."

"Let me think about it a bit more. I might be able to find a person to call on her. I could try to get some more information via Reza."

"But, Surreya, you have your own concerns! Don't put yourself in any more danger."

"There's no danger. I feel her pain like mine. I live myself in this nightmare and therefore I also want to be able to help her, if she wants help. Saving a young girl from captivity and sex slavery is a compassionate duty. Let me think about it."

"Does it feel easier now for you to meet Reza first and then your husband?"

"No, it's just as painful as the first few times. I feel bad feeling Reza's closeness, smell and body against me. But I have to cope with it and as long as he wants me, I have to obey him."

"Ugh, I feel so sorry for you and other women in your situation. I hope these men get their punishments one day." I felt how we encouraged each other to resist and fight. She was so strong in her soul that despite her own suffering, she wanted to save others.

Surreya helped rinse the washed bedding with cold water while we continued to talk.

"But I've thought about one thing and that's that you shouldn't be so curious about everyone. It can become dangerous for you. You are a young and inexperienced girl, Shemal."

"No, I'm careful and know what I'm doing. But I understand what you mean. Thank you for your consideration. When do you have visiting time next time?"

"In two weeks and I'll try to find more clues about Mahnaz. Is it okay if I show up like today when I need to talk to you?"

"Yes, but if my stepmother is home, we can't talk. But you can come, if we can talk we will, otherwise I will try to find an opportunity to contact you afterwards."

"That sounds good. I wish we could meet and talk whenever we want, but I understand your situation!"

"Goodbye, Shemal gyan."

Surreya hugged me and kissed my cheeks lovingly.

"Goodbye, Surreya, take care and be careful."

After Surreya left, I sat for a good while immersed in my thoughts.

When the laundry was done, I went to the home of the bonus grandparents and had a good lunch. Grandma was so good at cooking good food, and she loved food herself.

Stepmother came home and told me that my package of knitwear and my letter to Dad had been handed to him without any problems. I was so happy about it.

I had orders to sew and embroider bedding and curtains for a young girl who was getting married in a couple of weeks. I had to finish sewing everything in ten days, so I sat and worked day and night on it.

It had now been a week since I last met Surreya. The thought of Mahnaz and her situation kept spinning in my head. Could I help her?

***

All schools were still closed and the situation in the city was very bad. In the evenings there was a curfew and often we heard gunfire. It was said that there were clashes between regime forces and peshmerga groups just a few kilometers outside the city. We hoped that the peshmerga would liberate the city again. Life for all of us was much better before the Islamic regime occupied our cities.

I felt no joy in my everyday life any more and missed my father and my grandmother so much that I often cried in my loneliness. But I knew I had to be strong to help my little siblings and my stepmother in this difficult situation that we had ended up in. I had been unable to have any direct contact with my party comrades since the occupation of our city. But sometimes I got a letter from the party. Before the regime took over power in the city, I was very actively involved in a communist party, Cherik Fadaei. But my father was a long-time member of the Kurdistan Democratic party with the abbreviation PDKI. Before he was imprisoned, he had an important role and great responsibility both in the party and in the peshmerga group. Dad was arrested on the first night when Islamic regime forces managed to get the peshmerga out of the city at midnight. He was arrested in the morning at our home.

At the last moment before they brought him out, he gave me a secret mission. Handcuffed, dressed in his pajamas, he turned to me, who was sad and crying, and said in Kurdish.

"I'm not going away, you exist, and you know what I want. I trust you. Take care of your younger siblings. I know you can!"

After this incident, I left my communist ideology and joined my father's party, which was based on a social democratic ideology. I wanted to continue his political path and faith.

PDKI, I knew at a glance from the time my father was an active member. But I wanted more information about what the party's principles were like and how they worked on different issues. What was the party's view of the role of women? What were the party's statutes and regulations to work from? But when I joined the PDKI, under the rule and occupation of the Islamic regime in our area it was forbidden and deadly to have any material about political parties that belonged to the opposition. The party sent me, through the secret proxies they had in the city, letters in which I was updated on the peshmergas and the party's resistance activities in the area. They encouraged me to form small secret groups in the city to do certain underground missions, such as handing out party leaflets or delivering money and letters to peshmerga families.

The hard work and all the responsibility meant that I had repressed what I needed to feel good. I kept thinking about others, my dad, Grandma's death, Surreya and Mahnaz, had blocked all my feelings and own needs that a young girl should be allowed to have. Sometimes I felt like an old, fifty-year-old woman, but I never felt weak or like a victim! My dreams were my driving force. I dreamed of freedom, my father's freedom. That I would get the chance to educate myself. That I could achieve my goals in life. That I could help other women in need. These dreams gave me hope, strength and power to continue the struggle I had before me.

***

It was Friday and we were invited to Uncle's house for dinner and to sleep over with them. They had a home phone and I planned to find an opportunity to call Surreya from there. It had been almost two weeks since we last saw each other. We decided to walk there, it took fifteen minutes. Shoresh, my two-year-old little brother, refused to go and we didn't have a stroller for him. I carried him in my arms. He was heavy, but cozy and gooey. The other younger siblings walked hand in hand with our sister Nasrin.

Uncle's house was large with a farm with several fruit trees. It was arranged so that we could all sit on the carpet and pillows on the terrace. It was a warm and pleasant September evening. It was always nice to get there. Uncle and his family were very kind and caring to us and we felt at home with them.

I was especially happy that no one was inside the house. Then I could go in and make a call to Surreya!

After sitting there on the terrace for an hour, drinking tea and eating some nuts and cookies, I saw that the adults were very busy talking about different things and all the children were playing in the yard. I snuck into the hall and my cousin followed.

"Please, can you watch out for me for a short while? I need to make a call."

"You tell me who you're calling." She smiled.

"I'll tell you then, I promise."

"Okay go in, I'm standing in the kitchen guarding. Come out

as soon as I call out to you."

"Okay, thanks."

I stepped into the room and dialed Surreya's home phone number.

"Hello"

"Hey, Surreya, it's Shemal, how are you? Have you been to Orumiyeh?"

"I sent a letter about it the other day. Haven't you gotten it?"

"No, with whom did you send the letter?"

"Via the mother-in-law's nephew, who is ten years old. He said he had left it with your sister who would hand the letter to you."

"No, I haven't gotten it. I need to talk to my sister. I'll call you later tonight about it. But hope you're okay."

"Yes, it's business as usual, but some things have happened. We need to meet. Find the letter first."

"I hope you didn't write any important revelations in the letter. Nasrin is a little mischievous, she can gossip for her mother."

"No, no don't worry. I just wrote that I miss you and I want you to come and visit."

"Great, I'll call you then, bye."

I walked out of the room looking for my sister and found her in the yard.

"Nasrin, can you come, I need to talk to you."

"What do you want? Have I done something stupid?"

"No, come! I'm just going to ask something."

Nasrin came, a little worried, and we went into the phone room.

"Did you receive a letter from a ten-year-old boy the other day?"

"Nope... what boy?"

"Nasrin, I want you to tell me the truth. Then I won't get angry."

"Yes... Yes, just, I forgot to give that letter to you!"

"Where's the letter? What did you do with it?"

"I've hidden it! I forgot about it then!"

"Why are you doing that? Why didn't you come directly to me then?"

"Okay sorry! You'll get it when we get home."

"Have you told someone about it or shown the letter to your mother or anyone else?"

"No, I promise, I haven't."

"Okay, don't talk about it to anyone. Next time when someone leaves me a letter or other, you give it to me! Do we have an agreement?"

"Yes... sorry bajeh, big sister."

We went out to the others on the terrace, had a good dinner and hung out with Uncle's family.

Before it was time for everyone to come in and sleep, I called Surreya again.

"Hi, Surreya, yes, my little sister had received the letter from you and hidden it. She has vowed not to do so any more. I'm going to get it tomorrow, so don't worry."

"What a good thing, but why did she do it?"

"Oh, she's a little mischievous sometimes. When can we meet again?"

"You can decide. When can you come?"

"Maybe tomorrow afternoon. I'll make up an excuse to leave the kids for a while."

"Great, you're welcome whenever you show up."

I got the letter when we got home. Nasrin had hidden it under a rock in Grandpa's yard!

***

My sewing machine had messed up a bit in the last few days. I told my stepmother that I must show it to someone who can fix it. She agreed that I would take the sewing machine and walk away by myself without Shoresh this time.

At three o'clock in the afternoon the next day, I grabbed my sewing machine in a bag and walked away. On the way to Surreya's home, I felt a fear that someone was following me. I stopped and looked around several times but saw no one. Was I afraid that Stepmother wanted to know where to go and sent someone after me? Was I afraid that the regime's spies wanted to know who I met? I don't know. Maybe I was a little unnecessarily paranoid.

Arriving at Surreya's door, I rang the bell, and she was the one who opened.

"Hey, Shemal, gyan, welcome, come in."

"Thank you, are you alone or is your mother-in-law at home."

"No, she's not home. I've baked a good cake for us today."

"Thank you please, I'm so curious to hear what has happened?"

"I'll tell you, sit here. I will go and get the tea that I have prepared in the kitchen."

I sat on a pillow on the terrace. Surreya came out with a large tray full of sponge cake, tea and some fruit for us. It was both relaxing and nice that I could have a moment to myself and hang out and talk in peace with Surreya. I felt so good when I had these moments with her.

Surreya smiled at me and started talking.

"You'll see how good I've been. We women can do impossible things once we decide to do it. I received a phone call from Reza that I could go to Orumiyeh the day before the visiting time of my husband. He wanted me to spend a whole day with him before meeting Sirwan. He said he had fixed an apartment that belonged to one of his prison guard colleagues where we could stay for a day without being disturbed. I complained that he had told his friend about our relationship. Then he replied, naïve as he was:

"'All prison guards are like a chain. Everyone knows what the others are doing. We fix opportunities for each other and for our mullahs who are our bosses.'

"I then took the opportunity to ask if he and his colleagues knew how many other women Khalkhali had in his captivity. He got a little angry that I called it captivity but replied, 'Yes, we know that. We usually drive, shop and, if necessary, move them to other places. These women are not prisoners. They live a luxurious life for the services they provide to our bosses.'

"'Okay, can you show me how, for example, that Mahnaz lives luxuriously. I want to see it with my own eyes. If you ever want to give me such a suggestion, then I know what to expect!'

"'Yes, I can make sure you meet Mahnaz at her house. But you should be careful about talking in front of the older lady who lives with her. I'm going there with some goods tonight. I can tell Mahnaz that you will come with me and greet her. I will call you Maryam with her. Just for the sake of your safety. You see that I am doing everything to make you happy with me and our relationship. I'm starting to miss you between visits. I think I'm starting to fall in love with you, Surreya!'

"'So good Reza, I look forward to seeing what a luxurious

life Mahnaz has. I'm coming on Wednesday afternoon. Bye, see you soon.'

"'Don't forget that you're supposed to be made up and clean and dressed like a bride when you come to me. See you soon.'

"Reza used to call my father-in-law often before calling me at home. He had already told my father-in-law that he had arranged for Sirwan and me to spend a full two days together. My father-in-law bought a lot of fruits and nuts. My mother-in-law baked and made dolma, which is Sirwan's favorite food, to bring. I was ashamed and felt so guilty, when I saw how happy they were that Sirwan had such a good friend as Reza in prison. They sent both money and gifts through me to Reza.

"My father-in-law drove me to Orumiyeh and left me outside the prison as usual. He drove home and said that when Reza calls, he'll come and pick me up.

"I used to stand in line between the people in the crowd. Then, when the guards standing in the prison tower, saw me, a made-up woman with a colorful shawl on her head, they reported to Reza. He came out and called Sirwan's name and I went in. My makeup and shawl were the code that made the guards see me and Reza got a report that I was there.

"Reza picked me up through the main entrance to the prison and together we walked out through a back door to his car that was parked behind the house by the wall. He had already changed and was waiting to go out with me. We sat in his company car which was a Peykan with dark windows like pasdar's cars usually have. I asked why he didn't drive in his private car. He said it was safer that way, and that no one would stop a pasdar's car.

"I wasn't that familiar with the city of Orumiyeh and the streets there. But I noticed that he was driving a bit outside the city, until we arrived at a place which he said was Shekhtappa.

There were many newly built tall houses there. We stopped behind a house, and he parked the car. Then we walked in through the garage which was empty and took the elevator up to the fifth floor. Reza had a key, and he opened a door, which only said Gaffari.

"We went into a very nicely decorated living room. On the table was a platter of fruit. He showed me the kitchen which was a modern little kitchen. The bedroom was made up with red and white linens. A nice bathroom was next to the bedroom.

"I was so saddened by walking into an apartment with a man who wasn't mine and who was just taking advantage of me. I wished this apartment was mine and Sirwan's home. But just to save Sirwan's life, I exposed myself to all of this."

"I know, Surreya, I'm suffering with you. But you are brave, and you do it for your love. Hope that you soon can be reunited and that you will escape your suffering."

Surreya wiped her tears and wanted us to take a break to have tea.

"Good cake you've baked, thank you."

"I usually bake it when I visit Sirwan."

"Are you offering it to Reza too?"

"No, he knows it's just for Sirwan."

"And he respects that?"

"Yes, he does."

We looked at my sewing machine together and Surreya saw what the problem was. An underwire that had jammed and gotten rid of an underscrew like a wrapped lump. We pulled out and removed the sewing thread and put the screw back into the machine and the sewing machine worked as usual again. We had finished tea and I was eager to hear more.

"What happened next when you came into the apartment.

Did you get to meet Mahnaz?"

"Reza was like a hungry wolf and forced me to the bedroom first. He ripped off my clothes and attacked me again like an idiot. I went stiff and dull like a dead man, but he didn't care. He was so sex hungry. When he was satisfied, he fixed tea for the both of us. He explained that so that the lady in the house of Mahnaz would not be suspicious, he would introduce me as Maryam, his second wife! He said, 'Then you and Mahnaz can talk freely. But you must be careful and pretend to be my wife and not talk about other things.'

"He made a call first and then said we could walk home to Mahnaz. He also told me that he and I would be sleeping in this apartment tonight. I asked him what his wife would think if she knew what he was doing when he wasn't home at night.

"He replied very arrogantly that she had to be satisfied that she had food on the table, a roof over her head and a man to support her!

"We walked a few houses away to a high-rise that was lower than the one we were in. We took the elevator to the third floor. He rang a door that said only Reza A lady fully covered with black chador opened. Reza said his greetings and told the lady that he was the ayatollah's official with his wife.

"'Ayatollah Khalkhali has offered my wife Maryam to meet his wife here.'

"The older lady knew exactly what he meant. She said, 'Your wife is welcome, but men are not allowed in because we are only women in here.'

"Reza replied that it was just right, and he wasn't going to come in either. He left me and said he would come and pick me up in two hours. The lady let me in, and I entered a lounge that was their living room. It was decorated like rooms you see on movies, with luxurious furniture, tables and large mirrors on the walls. Several candlesticks were placed in different corners and on tables in the hall. A large, elegant crystal chandelier hung from the ceiling. I had to sit on the couch for a while before she picked up Mahnaz from the bedroom.

"When Mahnaz entered the room, I felt fear, dizziness, and nausea. She was a rather tall slender, pale young girl. I immediately understood that she had smoked tiriac. Her eyes were dull, red and lifeless. She was wearing a long green floral long-arm dress. Her blonde hair was braided, and two long thick braids hung on each side of her breasts. She was, despite the unnatural pallor, beautiful as a flower. She took slow steps towards me. I could see that her gait wasn't normal. She had no strength in her legs.

"She sat down on the couch across from me.

"'Hi, my name is Maryam, nice to meet you. My husband and your husband are close at work and so I come to visit you today. How are you?'

"'Hi, Maryam, khanum, you're welcome. I have a bit of a headache and am lethargic because of it. You'll have to excuse me.'

"The old lady came in with a tray of tea, cold drink and a special drink in a glass to Mahnaz. She left us and went to the kitchen.

"'Do you speak Kurdish?'

"She signaled that she was afraid of the older lady who was her supervisor in the house.

"'Yes, but we're just talking Farsi here.' She pointed cautiously at the lady in the kitchen and said that she reported everything to Khalkhali!

"'Yes, of course, we're just talking Farsi!' With my eyes, I confirmed to Mahnaz that I understood her fears.

"I drank tea and took a piece of melon. But Mahnaz only took a few sips of her special drink out of the glass. I noticed that she became more alert after a while. She could smile and show joy.

"I didn't dare ask much. I let her talk. She asked, 'How long have you been married to your husband?' She meant Reza!

"I became tearful and swallowed my crying in my throat.

"'One year. What about you?'

"'I've lived here for ten months.' She turned and looked after the old lady. She was nowhere to be seen.

"'When did you marry Ayatollah?'

"'Ten months ago.' She stared at me.

"I felt like I was starting to feel bad about not being able to talk freely and having to play fake. I saw that Mahnaz suspected that I was also a victim like her. Her eyes wanted to say so much, but her mouth was closed.

"'Do you have wedding pictures or albums? You're so beautiful, I'm curious how beautiful you must have been when you were dressed and made up as a bride.'

"She smiled and shook her head.

"'There was no wedding for me. But I have a photo album in the bedroom that I can show you.'

"Mahnaz went into the bedroom, and I got up to go to the bathroom. The bathroom door was closed, and I heard that the older lady was in there washing herself.

"I quickly went into Mahnaz's bedroom and left the note with my phone number for her and said in Kurdish:

"'I know who you are. Me and you have the same fate. Can you try calling me on this number so we can talk?'

"'Next week I get to travel to my mother and siblings in

Mahabad. Then I can call you from there.'

"'Great, we keep acting like we don't know anything about each other.'

"'Okay, go back to the hall.'

"I quickly went back to my couch and started eating another piece of melon. The lady came out of the bathroom and asked where Khanum was.

"'Don't know, she went in that direction.'

"She walked quickly toward Mahnaz's bedroom.

"A few minutes later, they both came out and sat with me in the living room.

"I politely asked the older lady, 'Are you related to Ayatollah Khalkhali?'

"'Yes, you could say that. I count as his aunt. I'm a widow and my adult children don't want me. I work and live here with the khanum and hazrate Ayatollah.'

"I could hear her Azeri accent as she spoke Farsi.

"'How kind hazrate Ayatollah is. May God preserve him for you and everyone he helps!'

"'Amen,' Mahnaz said, looking at me with a strange look.

I was ashamed inside that I was praying for a sadistic mullah who enjoyed executing innocent people.

"Mahnaz showed me a photo album with pictures from her childhood with her parents and younger siblings. There were no pictures of her and her husband, the ayatollah!

"I saw that her father and mother in one picture were wearing Kurdish clothes. Mahnaz looked for a good while at the picture of her father. She ran her finger over the picture and sighed deeply. I felt a pressure in my chest and a lump in my throat. We looked at each other and both noticed that our tears were running down our cheeks. It was a good thing that the older lady was in the kitchen. Mahnaz pointed to the picture and to her heart and I nodded that I understood. I wished I could hug her and that we could cry against each other's shoulders. I gently whispered that she had to call me when she was with her family in Mahabad. She confirmed it with her eyes and her hand on her heart.

"Time passed quickly, I thought I had only been there for half an hour, when we heard the intercom ring. The older lady replied briefly and hung up. She came up to me and said it was my husband.

"'He wants you to come down to go home.'

"I hugged Mahnaz and whispered again that I would wait for her call. I hugged the lady too and said it was nice and that they were welcome to visit us."

"Oh, you've succeeded! Has Mahnaz called?"

"No, not yet, but she will. I saw it on her that she wanted to talk to me, but she was scared. She just needs the right opportunity."

"What did Reza say afterwards? How did you manage all night with him?"

"He had bought some food and he ate everything himself. I was so affected by the situation and felt bad. I lied to Reza and said that the older lady offered dolma, which I ate a lot of. After dinner, he lit a hookah and put a lump of black dough on the lighter, drawing deep flares. I think it was tiriac. He became lethargic but happy afterwards. He put on a cassette in the tape recorder and wanted me to dance for him.

"I reluctantly tried to dance a little bit. Then I noticed that he had already fallen asleep. I was so happy and prayed to God that he would not be awake all night. I put out the fire in the hookah. I had the urge to take a knife from the kitchen and cut him into pieces, but the thought of them killing Sirwan stopped me. I went to bed in my clothes on the couch and fell asleep. In the morning, he had a headache and felt unwell. I made some tea, and we had breakfast, but he couldn't eat. He wanted us to drive back to prison. He needed to be given painkillers by the nurse there.

"He left me in the room in the prison house and locked the door from the outside. I fell asleep and woke up to the fact that he had come back in. He said he wasn't feeling well and was poisoned by what he smoked the night before. He said he had ordered another prison guard to bring Sirwan to me in the room in an hour. We got to be together until the next day, at twelve o'clock. Reza said that if we didn't see each other tomorrow, he would call later. He would plan better nights together for us. I thanked God that I didn't have to suffer a long night. I also prayed to God that Reza would die of poisoning so that I wouldn't have to see him again.

"Sirwan and I had a nice night together. We ate, talked, and slept closely in each other's arms in the small prison bed."

"Surreya, you are a very brave woman. I hope you can save yourself and even Mahnaz from this hell. I admire you."

"You know I'm living just for Sirwan's sake. I must fight and do everything for him and his life."

"I know that, my friend, and I see that the love of Sirwan gives you the courage and power to fight on."

"Sorry I have to go now, but please keep in touch with me! Let me know when Mahnaz gets in touch."

"I'm so grateful that you're there for me, Shemal gyan. Rest assured; I'll tell you when I know something new."

We hugged each other and I went home with a lot of things on my mind.

***

It had been a week since I had been at Surreya's house. My uncle showed up in the afternoon and wanted me to accompany him to Orumiyeh the very next day to visit Dad. He told us that we would then drive to Tabriz to meet a responsible and close contact of Ayatollah Montazeri. Ayatollah Montazeri was after Ayatollah Khomeini number two in the hierarchy of the Islamic regime. My uncle said he had learned through contacts that a letter from Montazeri to Khalkhali could pardon my father from his death sentence. I was frightened and shuddered throughout my body: "What if this contact has plans to bring me to some mullah and subject me to the same fate as Mahnaz?"

I asked my uncle:

"Why do I have to join? Why not Stepmother this time?"

"Because she can't speak Farsi and she's not good at talking to anyone at all! You're his daughter and you're good at speaking for you. But you should not argue. You should ask them to help. Your father has suggested that instead of his wife, you should be there to talk for him."

"I'm afraid to meet people like that!"

"If you're doing the 'right way', you don't have to be afraid. What are you afraid of?"

"These men are disgusting and unscrupulous."

"I understand what you mean, but now it's about your father's life and death. We'll have to do everything we can."

I fell silent. I saw Mahnaz in front of me, the image of her that Surreya had described. I froze and got a feeling of discomfort. Uncle wanted me to go in and pack a small bag with what I needed for a few days of travel.

Early in the morning the next day, I was in the car with Uncle. I wasn't happy about this trip.

"What are you so afraid of, Shemal?" asked Uncle.

"I don't know, but I don't like meeting mullahs and the men around them."

"But you can show by the way you behave that you are stronger than them. But show no resistance to them! And don't show that you're politically savvy!"

"Then how am I going to show that I'm stronger than them as you say?"

"You can tell them about how hard you kids have it without your father. Ask them to feel sorry for the children."

"But, Uncle, you know I can't do that. I will unconsciously be aggressive towards them. You know I hate them. Why do you take me to such a meeting?"

"Okay, take it easy. You get to talk to them as you like. But there is a risk that they will imprison you too!"

"But we're going to pay a lot of money. We're going to bribe them, aren't we? It will be a buy-and-sell call. A negotiation that we pay so much to get a letter from that mullah about amnesty for Dad's sentence. If so, let me be a negotiator, not a beggar!"

"Okay, you're allowed to be a negotiator, but you have to hide your hatred for them. Try to be a little soft in the conversation and do not show aggression."

"I'll try, but don't interrupt. Otherwise, there is a risk that I will lose the thread and have an outburst. Does Dad know what we're going to do?"

"I can't talk to him openly about it. But I'm talking in codes about crops and fruits that are going to ripen. I think he understands what I'm talking about."

"Uncle, you absolutely must not leave me alone with them, even if they request it. Then you say no! All right?"

"There's no reason you should sit alone with anyone. I

promise I'll be with you all the time."

We arrived in Orumiyeh early in the morning. We parked the car in a remote car park and walked towards the prison house.

I started having palpitations again. I saw that many people were already standing outside the prison waiting. This time I had decided not to go around looking at people. I was afraid to meet any more like Surreya and that I wouldn't be able to cope with more stories of this kind. So, I focused on the visit to my dad and thought about what to say to him. I didn't want to make him feel worse than he already did. Dad was very saddened by Grandma's death, and he mourned her passing deeply.

We took a seat in a corner where several others stood waiting.

My restlessness began again. I had a hard time standing still and my legs wouldn't obey me. I took small steps up and down standing in place. Uncle asked me to stand still, but I couldn't.

"I have to sit or walk around."

Uncle became angry.

"You're going to put us in trouble. Why can't you, like everyone else, stand still and wait?"

"I try but my legs don't obey me. I'm nervous and restless, Uncle." I got tears in my eyes and struggled not to let the tears flow.

"Okay, go to the back where people are standing and take small steps around there."

I left him and walked through the crowd to take a seat at the back.

An old woman took my hand and pulled me towards her. I stopped and saw that there was an elderly man standing next to her, both wearing Kurdish clothes. I greeted in Kurdish.

"Hi, daya, what can I help with?"

"We're illiterate, and we can't speak Farsi. Can you help us and write answers to these questions?" She showed me a form they had been given to fill out.

I looked at the form and there were some simple questions about their name, age and address as parents of the daughter who was in prison. I took them to the back to sit along the wall and fill out the form for them.

"Daya, what's the name of your daughter who's inside the prison?"

"Kajal Mokhtari, my daughter, she is only seventeen." Daya began to cry. Her husband took over.

"I'll answer the questions, my daughter."

"Okay, Uncle, what's your name and daya's? How old are you?"

"I'm sixty-six years old and my wife Fatm is fifty-six. Our daughter Kajal is seventeen years old, and she is our youngest child."

"When was Kajal imprisoned? Why?"

"She was jailed five months ago, and we haven't been able to see her. Her three brothers are peshmerga in the mountains. She hasn't done anything. She's just a kid and was at home all the time. We don't know why they have imprisoned her."

"What is your address? Where do you live?"

"We live in Qalatan, a village near Khaneh."

I filled out the form for them and when I wanted to leave, she held my arm again and pulled me towards her. She was still crying and showed me a picture of her daughter Kajal, a cute young girl. Daya asked me to help them when their name or daughter's name was called by the guards. I promised to do it. I took them with me towards where my uncle was waiting. Uncle became pensive and with his eyes asked me what I was up to now.

"Why do you have them with you?"

"Uncle, it's Daya Fatm and Uncle Smaeil. They can't read and write and don't speak Farsi either. We'll help them talk to the prison guards when it's their turn."

Uncle's mimicry showed his displeasure, but he was forced to accept.

"Yes, okay, hey you. Come and stand here with me. Inshalla, it will soon be your turn."

I stood with them for a while and as soon as I moved, my uncle reacted and ordered me to remain here. "You're not going anywhere!" He was afraid that I would pick more help-seeking people among the people for us.

The old lady chatted with her God and prayed all the time. She was only fifty-six years old but looked as wrinkled and worn out as an eighty-year-old. I stepped closer and held her arm.

"Daya are you tired, do you want to sit for a bit?"

"Yes, my daughter, I have so much pain in my back but there is nothing to sit on here."

I saw that a younger man had a small wooden stool with him. I walked over and asked to borrow it for a little while. I showed her over there and said that she had back pain. He handed it to me. I came back and got the old lady to sit on the stool and I stood in support of her back to lean on.

She sighed and thanked her God and then me! She said that her daughter was also like me, a kind and sweet girl.

We had been standing for over an hour when the speakers started sounding. The sound created worries and movement in the waiting crowd. Even though they knew that it didn't matter where they stood, the guards would come to read the names of the prisoners who had visiting hours. But everyone wanted to come forward and stand near the entrance to the prison.

From the loudspeaker, I heard the name Kajal Mokhtari being shouted. I held daya in her arm and helped her up.

"Now it's your turn. They shouted Kajal's name."

We hurried towards the door. Kajal's father reached the prison guard and showed his completed paper. Daya and I came after. The guard asked me because he had understood that none of them understood Farsi.

"Who are you? Are you their daughter?"

"No, I just want to help because they can't speak Farsi and don't understand Azeri either."

"But you're not allowed to come in. Tell them we can pick up one of my colleagues who speaks Kurdish in there."

I translated for the old couple. They thanked me and followed the prison guard in.

I went back to my uncle. He looked at me a little angrily.

"It's good to help people, but we ourselves have problems and that's why we're standing here. I don't want you to go around picking up people like this with you. We don't know these people. They might cooperate with the regime!"

"No, Uncle, not these poor people. But I understand your fear. Okay, I'm standing here with you."

We heard my father's name being called.

"Ahmad Kamrani."

We walked over, showed identity cards and followed the guard who showed the way.

We passed a long semi-dark corridor, turned right to another. At the top of the corridor's end, a large metal door opened. We stepped back into another rather dark corridor. I again saw the long wall of glass windows. We were placed at a window in the middle of the corridor. We waited a long while for Dad to come up on the inside and talk to us on the outside of the thick glass wall.

I saw Dad come forward. A guard held his arm. He was wearing the knitwear I'd made for him. His bruises around his eyes and cheek were yellow green now. He smiled when he saw us on the other side. We were given signs by the guard to lift the gray phone. I took it first.

"Hey, Dad, how are you?"

"Good, my daughter, thank you for these warm and comfortable clothes you've knitted for me. I can smell them. I feel your presence with me all the time. Are your younger siblings doing well?"

"Yes, everyone's fine. Stepmother greets and she feels good in her pregnancy too."

Dad shook his head, and I interpreted it as his dissatisfaction with his wife's pregnancy this time.

"Dad is there anything more you need that I can arrange?"

"No, my daughter, that's fine."

My uncle took the phone away from me.

"Hey, Ahmad, how are you? I will come next time, inshalla, with good fruits for you. I'm going to Tabriz to buy the best fruits there and take them with me."

Now I understood that Uncle was trying to give good news to Dad. It was about our journey and contact with Ayatollah Montazeri and the letter to Khalkhali with amnesty for his death sentence. I read my dad's lips behind the thick glass where he just said, Inshalla... Inshalla... Inshalla.

Time ran out and then the phone fell silent. Uncle sighed and hung up the phone. We waved to Dad, and he looked at us until we disappeared from his sight.

We were let out through the same corridors we entered

through. Outside, I wanted to see if the older couple had come out. Without asking Uncle, I walked straight towards the waiting crowd again. I looked around but didn't find them. I turned to the main entrance disappointedly to see if my uncle was standing there waiting for me. I was delighted when I saw that he was standing with the old couple talking to them and I quickly walked over.

"Hi, Daya Fatm, how did it go. How is Kajal doing?"

She cried and couldn't speak. Her husband also wiped his cheeks and nose.

"She's not going to be able to cope with this. She's going to die. She's skinny as a stick. They have tortured her. She couldn't walk and could barely speak."

They both cried inconsolably. I asked if we could give them a ride somewhere. I didn't look at Uncle in case he showed displeasure!

But Uncle confirmed it with me and said: "I'll go get the car. You can wait here with Shemal. I'll be here soon." He walked towards the car.

The three of us took small steps towards the road while daya held onto my arm. She fought for every step she took forward.

Uncle came with the car. I helped daya sit in the back and asked her husband to sit in the front. She sat with me in the back seat holding my hand and crying the whole time.

Uncle drove to a restaurant outside the city. He offered lunch and told us all to eat and rest for a bit before he would drive them to the main bus terminal.

Without us asking, Kajal's father began to tell us.

"We have three sons who are peshmerga at Komala and we have not seen them since the regime took over our area. Our daughter was very sad when her brothers disappeared. She also wanted to become a peshmerga and flee to the border areas. But her mother was so sad and sick when she heard that, so Kajal stayed instead to be able to take care of her mother. She was always at home with her mother. We don't understand why they have arrested her."

"What did she say today when you met her? Has she received any judgement?" I asked.

"She was so terrified and tired. She just cried and didn't say anything. We saw on her face that they had beaten her and tortured her."

They cried again. My uncle was sad, quiet, and didn't say much. I was again so full of hatred for the regime and felt like a ticking time bomb that could explode any minute. But I tried to be calm and comfort the old couple instead of sprinkling salt in their wounds.

After we had eaten and drunk our tea, we drove the old couple to the bus terminal, so they could go home. My uncle walked over and bought their tickets. We could see that they were poor. We left some of the cookies and drinks we brought for them to have along the way.

Every time I came here to the prison, it became a new sadness for me. Now I couldn't help but think of Kajal and her parents. What a life we Kurds now had after the revolution. We thought that everything would be better, but already only a year after the revolution everything had become so much worse.

***

Uncle and I drove towards Tabriz, the second largest city in Iran. It is known as a city for Azeris. Many of the Islamic mullahs come from Tabriz. We were to meet a man who would get us in contact with Ayatollah Montazeri, who was a mullah in the inner circle of the Islamic regime with great power.

Uncle had sold all our land, our orchard and the gold we had, to get enough money to pay as bribes. Maybe we should meet Ayatollah Montazeri ourselves, otherwise it would be through his assistant.

We were both quiet and pensive. I had a hard time just thinking about what was going to happen in the near future. I had different scenarios and thoughts in my head. "How am I going to talk to those we're going to meet. When could I call Surreya to find out what has happened? Has Mahnaz called her? Has Reza asked for her again?"

I asked my uncle, "What do you think will happen to the old couple's daughter in prison?"

"She'll certainly be executed if they don't get her to confess or spy for them. Or she'll die of hunger and under torture."

"Ugh, Uncle don't say that. Then her old mother will die of grief or a heart attack."

"Yes, like your grandmother who died of stress and a heart attack on a bus on the way to Orumiyeh. Unfortunately, many Kurdish mothers will die when they hear how the regime captures and slaughters their children. It is the fate of the Kurds."

"I hate this regime and everyone who works for it. I want to be peshmerga and fight them."

"Easy, just take it easy. You are needed to save your own father right now. Your siblings need you. It wouldn't be good if you were to leave everything and everyone just for your hatred of the regime. What you're doing now is also a struggle."

I thought and confirmed what he said.

"It's true, my dad would be disappointed in me if I left my younger siblings alone."

I became silent and pensive again. Uncle became worried and asked, "Hmm... why did you get so quiet?"

"I'm thinking. It's true what you're saying. I'm not leaving my family and Dad in his mourning."

"Bravo, now you are a wise and wise girl. We will soon arrive in Tabriz. We will visit an acquaintance of mine who knows our destination with the trip here. He's going to help us with various practical things here."

"Is he one of the regime's men?"

"No, he's a retired officer from the Shah's time. He and his family are Azeri, but they are Kurdish-friendly. They've known me and your father for a long time. Tomorrow, he will take us to an office belonging to Ayatollah Montazeri. There we will meet a man named Farshid Mohammadi, who is the right hand of the ayatollah. I hope he can help us meet the ayatollah tomorrow. I'm more worried about each day that passes by. You also hear that Khalkhali executes political prisoners on a daily basis."

"Yes, I hear that. I'm also very worried about Dad."

"That's why you and I have to be humble and ask for help. Do not show hatred and resistance!"

"Okay, Uncle, I understand that. Do not be alarmed, I will take care of it in the best way. I beg you again that you do not leave me alone with them!"

We spent the night at Uncle's acquaintance's house. They were kind and respectful. Now we were on our way to the office where we were to meet Farshid Mohammadi. I was nervous and had a little tingle in my stomach. But I knew how to behave. I had to borrow a chador from our host's wife. Now I had both a long coat that went below the knee, veil and an all-over black chador on me. Only the eyes with my glasses were visible.

We were stopped at the gate. I was directed to the women's

corridor for body searches. Several women with full-face black chador sat there. They searched my entire body and then let me in.

I met my uncle in the middle of a large hall, where we were waiting for someone to come and show us into Farshid Mohammadi's office.

We followed an Islamic militiaman, who was our guide, and entered a room. There sat a man, in civilian clothes with a shirt and a pair of trousers. He didn't seem to be a mullah himself. Behind him was a large picture of Ayatollah Khomeini and Montazeri on the wall. In the corner there was a large standing Iranian flag with Islamic texts in Arabic.

The man behind the table showed us two chairs some distance away from his table. Without introducing himself, he said, "What can I do for you?"

My uncle walked over and put an envelope on his table and backed towards his chair.

He quickly looked at the contents of the envelope and saw that it was a ton of money. He had a hidden smile on his face as he put the envelope in his desk cupboard.

In a slightly trembling voice, my uncle began to talk.

"Qurban, this is my niece, the oldest of six children. We are here to ask for help so that a father of six gets amnesty on his sentence."

"In what prison is your brother? What is he convicted of?"

"He's in Orumiyeh prison. We've only heard of his verdict. We have not received anything in writing."

"Was he against the Islamic Revolution?"

I answered that question.

"He and we are Kurds and, as you know, all Kurds today are suspected of being Zedeh Enqelab. My father is labeled as Zedeh

Enqelab."

"Was he a Democrat or a Komala?"

"Democrat."

Uncle was completely silent.

Farshid looked in his notebook which certainly contained the names and phone numbers of the people he needed to call. He picked up the phone and made a call.

"Allo, Qurban, relatives of a Kamrani who is in the prison in Orumiyeh are here. Can I arrange for them to meet Hazreteh Ayatollah?"

He hung up the phone and wanted us to go with him to another office in the house.

We were seated in a small waiting room outside a larger office on the third floor. Our contact went in to talk to Ayatollah Montazeri who we hoped would write the letter for us.

He came out and wanted us to go into the mullah ourselves. I pulled down my chador and also covered my mouth and nose.

Inside the large office, the mullah sat behind a giant empty desk with only a Koran in the right corner of the table and a pad with a pencil in front of him. We each sat on a chair in a row of chairs against the wall at a considerable distance from him. He welcomed us and asked me first.

"What can I help you with, my daughter?"

"Bismillahe Rahmaneh Rahim, Jenabeh Ayatollah, my father is arrested by your men and is in prison. We are six children, and my mother is pregnant with the seventh child. Our big house with everything we had was confiscated after my father's arrest. We now live as a poor family. My father is under the threat of being executed. I ask you to be a saving angel for us six children so that we do not lose our father."

"Why was your father arrested? Was he Zedeh Enqelab?"

"Hazreteh Ayatollah, when the revolution in Iran began, my father, in our city of Piranshar, was the one who led all the demonstrations against the Shah's regime. You know that when the Shah left Iran, we formed our own autonomous government in our Kurdish areas.

"It was something that Ayatollah Khomeini had approved and promised that the Kurdish parts of Iran would have their own rule. But when Islamic forces took power in our cities, all those involved in the implementation of the revolution and in the Kurdish autonomous rule were branded as Zedeh Enqelab, against the revolution. They were imprisoned and many were executed."

I cried and continued, "My father has all his life been a person who has helped the poor, orphans and those who needed help. He is not an evil man."

"Is he a Muslim?"

"He was born Muslim, but he was never a man of faith. His faith is his love of humanity."

He fell silent for a good while and then he asked me again.

"How can I contribute?"

"By a letter to Ayatollah Khalkhali, that he will not execute my father before he gets his verdict at a trial."

"But no one can execute someone until they get a verdict through the Islamic court!"

"I hope you know what's going on in Orumiyeh prison. Every day, twenty or so people are killed without judgment. A week ago, Ayatollah Khalkhali gave the order to execute fifty-nine people who had received no verdict!"

He fell silent again and wrote something on his pad. My uncle was pale with fear. He didn't dare to look at me. He was angry and scared.

I wasn't scared but felt that I had managed to influence the mullah behind the table.

He rang a bell. The man who guided us came in. The mullah told him.

"Get my stationery and my stamp."

He walked towards a corner cabinet in the room that was locked that he had a key to. He retrieved a paper folder and a drawer from the cupboard and came back to the mullah's table.

"Wait here," the mullah told him.

The ayatollah began to write. I looked at my uncle to get a kind look and confirmation that things are going in the right direction. But he just looked at the mullah and was petrified.

The ayatollah signed and stamped the letter. He asked the man standing next to him to read it to us.

Bismillahe Rahmaneh Rahim, Hazrateheh Ayatollah Khalkhali.

I have today granted amnesty to Ahmad Kamrani who is a political prisoner in Orumiyeh. I order you to execute the amnesty. He must not end up among those who are executed. His sentence may be twenty years in prison. I will follow his case personally through my representative in Orumiyeh.

With respect

Ayatollah Mohammad Montazeri

My uncle stepped forward, bent over to leave another thick envelope, and kissed the back of the mullah's hand in thanks. I remained seated on my chair.

Ayatollah quickly checked the contents of the envelope and then put it in the box under his table. He turned to my uncle and said:

"Tell your brother that I pardon him for the sake of his children. I hope he gets educated as a faithful and loyal Muslim man in prison."

He turned to me and said:

"My daughter, you are a good speaker and you made me write this letter without hesitation. May God help you and your father."

"Thank you, Hazreteh Ayatollah, for your compassionate actions. I hope many in power think like you, God preserve you."

At the same time, I was ashamed inside that I was talking to and praying for a mullah.

We were shown out by the same man. We walked to the car that was standing in a parking lot a street away. Uncle had gotten some color back on his face, and I couldn't help but ask a stupid question.

"It went well, Uncle. Why were you so scared and silent all the time?"

"I was very scared when you started talking about Kurds and autonomy. Did you forget that he is also a mullah and against Kurds. He could have put you in jail too. You talked politics with him. I was about to have a heart attack!"

"No, I just informed him of the crazy things Khalkhali is doing in Orumiyeh. You saw he was affected. How much money did he get? How much was in the envelope you gave him?"

"You don't want to know that. You don't."

"No, I have to know, it's mine and my siblings' money. You see how I struggle to have money for the basic everyday needs of my family."

"Yes, I know that. But we are doing everything possible to save your father's life!"

"Yes, absolutely. But I want to know how much you gave in the two envelopes?"

"I gave the contact man three million tuman and to the

ayatollah ten million tuman. But it was worth it. We must urgently hand over this letter personally to Khalkhali."

"I refuse to give it to him. You and Stepmother can do it."

"Why? Look how you could influence this ayatollah. You might succeed just as well with Khalkhali."

"Uncle, if it's going to cost my father's death, I refuse to see Khalkhali. I hope you understand what I'm saying."

"Okay, take it easy. Think about it. We can talk about it when we get home."

"No, we've finished talking about it. I'm not thinking. I hate that human butcher and never want to be around him. Stop pushing me and don't mention it to my stepmother. We decide here and now that you and she go to this Satan and leave the letter."

"Okay, Shemal, I know how stubborn you are. I hear what you're saying. No one can force you."

Before we drove away, we bought some food to eat in the car on the way home.

Uncle drove for three and a half hours without a break and without us talking to each other.

I thought of poor Mahnaz who must be in bed with this old Satan mullah, Khalkhali. If she had been as stubborn as I was and refused to agree. But I don't know if she would have agreed to it or been forced to do it.

I really wanted to meet her and help her escape the nightmare she's living in.

***

We came to Shno where my uncle lived with his family. He was going to drive me home to Khaneh tomorrow. It was fun to meet my cousins and especially she who was the same age as me. We were very close, but I didn't share my political secrets with her. She was scared and could reveal them. I loved her very much. At my uncle's house, there was a home phone that I asked my cousin to pick up to her room when everyone had gone to bed. I needed to make a call. She smiled and said:

"I know who you want to call."

"Well, who?"

"To Shanga, the one you're in love with."

"Yes, quite right. Can you watch out for me when I call?"

"Yes, of course."

It was ten o'clock in the evening, and uncle and Aunt had gone to bed. But my three mischievous younger cousins were still playing. I asked their big sister to look after them and not let them come in when I used the phone. I cautiously walked into her room, picked up the phone and dialed Surreya's number. She answered instantly.

"Hi, Surreya, sorry to call so late. But I'm in Shno calling from my uncle's home phone. How are you?"

"Hey, Shemal gyan, I've missed you. We need to meet. I have a lot to tell."

"I'm coming home tomorrow morning. I'm going to ask my uncle to leave me in town. Then I'll go straight to your house. Is that okay?"

"Yes perfect, we can have lunch together, then you can go home in the afternoon."

"we'll say so. Good night."

At night, I slept in my cousin's room on a mattress. We talked girltalk anyway until dawn.

The next day, at ten o'clock after breakfast, my uncle said that he would drive me first to Khaneh, which is only forty kilometers away from Shno, then he would go to his appliance store and work. Before we arrived, I asked him:

"Can you leave me in town, I haven't been able to see a friend lately. I don't feel good and need to see a friend. But my stepmother cannot be told."

"How do I know it's a friend you're dating…? Hehe…" Uncle smiled.

"I promise it's a girlfriend. Don't you trust me?"

"Well then, I'm just kidding. I know you're having a tough time. I'll leave you where you want."

"Thank you, Uncle."

It was ten past eleven o'clock in the morning when I rang the door at Surreya's. I was happy and at the same time excited to hear what had happened.

"Hey, come in." Surreya hugged me.

"How are you? Are you alone?"

"Yes, all alone."

We went into the kitchen, picked up the tray with everything we needed for lunch for the living room that was adjacent to the kitchen. We set the table for two on a canvas on the floor. Surreya took the saucepan with the food and placed it in the middle. The lovely aroma of a tomato soup with basil spread.

"Go ahead, we eat and talk at the same time." Surreya smiled.

"Tell me, have you met Mahnaz?"

"No, but we've talked on the phone three times. We have a plan to meet.

"She called a week after I had been with her in Orumiyeh. She was visiting her family in Mahabad. She was afraid that their home phone would be bugged by the regime. Therefore, she called from a neighbor's home phone. She said she was forced to agree to become Khalkhali's siga wife because then he would make sure her father would not be executed. She said that from the very first night, Khalkhali had forced her to smoke tiriac, in order to cope with sleeping with him.

"She remembered nothing from the first night with him more than that the next day she had a lot of pain in her lower abdomen and bled for several days. She had a headache, was nauseous, and vomited several times. Since then, the lady who suited her at home has given her some medicine dissolved in a glass of juice or lemonade a couple of times a day. This meant that she could not think clearly or be sad and she did not feel any pain in her body. The lady forced her to drink the whole glass as well as to eat food afterwards."

"Has Mahnaz been allowed to meet her father in prison?"

"Yes, with her mother. But he does not know that his daughter is a sex slave of Khalkhali to save his life."

"But how could this happen to her? How did Khalkhali catch an eye on her?"

"Of course, through the special prison guards he has there. Her father was a peshmerga and had snuck into town to see his wife and the children. Some spy had figured it out and sent a group of Islamic militias to their meeting point where he was arrested. Her father, like all other Kurdish prisoners, ended up in the prison in Orumiyeh and a day later he received his execution sentence. Mahnaz and her mother were referred to meet Khalkhali to ask for a pardon.

"When they met him, he became very interested in Mahnaz. He made his demand that if the girl married him, he would make sure her father escaped his execution sentence. Mahnaz's mother immediately said yes to it without even asking her daughter!

"She signed a paper that she would make sure Mahnaz

became his siga wife, and no one would know. Relatives and neighbors would be told that Mahnaz lived with her uncle in Tehran and went to school there! A week later, Mahnaz's mother left her in Orumiyeh, in the house she would live in and become Khalkhali's siga wife. Her father's death sentence was changed to twenty years in prison."

"Oh my God, how cruel can a human being be? He is at least forty years older than her. Poor Mahnaz. But how does she cope with him?"

"She's drugged all the time. An IUD has been inserted into her so that she does not get pregnant. She said she feels like a dead person. She lives so her father could live. She has no choice, just like me. She wants me to visit her often, but I'm terrified of it. If the lady who lives with her figures out what we're talking about or hear that we're talking Kurdish, then that's it for all of us. She can only call me when she's visiting her family every two months. I have promised her that next time when she is in Mahabad I will visit her. She will tell her mother that we are in the same situation, and therefore need to support each other."

"Isn't there a risk that her mother could leak information about you to Khalkhali or Reza? She might be spying for them."

"Yes, you're right. But we have no other chance to be able to meet."

"I think you should double-check it with Mahnaz before you go there."

"I'll do that, wise thought. I have to ask Reza again. Then, of course, I have to spend a whole night with him for that. You went and met your father. How is he?"

"Yes, I did, along with my uncle. He feels better compared to the last visit. But he's also worried, like us, about what's going to happen to him. Surreya, I am so worried about you and about

Mahnaz that I sometimes forget my father. Unfortunately, I can't help you in any other way than just listening. Let me know if I can contribute in any way!"

"You should take care of yourself and not let yourself end up in our situation. There are certainly several dozen other women who are in our situation and perhaps worse. We must fight on for the lives of our loved ones. That I am able to talk to you and share my burden with you without being afraid means so much to me. I feel like I'm gaining more strength from meeting you."

"I have to go home now. But I'll call you as soon as I get a chance." You can try to reach me if something more happens. Be careful with Mahnaz and her mother."

We hugged and I left her once again with a heavy feeling in my chest and lots of thoughts.

***

My stepmother's belly grew, and the stress increased over how we could handle her delivery and a newborn baby in the cramped accommodation.

I had recently managed to meet two party comrades and had a meeting with them in a secret place. They commissioned me to carry out some resistance activities, partly to share leaflets, partly to have meetings with some supporters in the city and carry out missions with them.

It was late fall and still no schools were open. Both schoolchildren, adolescents and adults felt very bad. In the city, armed regime forces, regime militias, pasdar were constantly patrolling. Fear of being arrested or killed prevailed. Almost every family in the city had lost one family member and had one or two incarcerated. The concern that the detainees would be executed was so great that it affected people's mental well-being on a daily basis. Everyone kept listening to the local radio to see if their incarcerated relatives were on lists of those executed.

Our life had gotten much worse. My stepmother had a boy three days earlier, and the cost of living for us had increased. I worked even harder sewing and embroidering to make a little more money.

My father was still in prison. Lately, only Uncle had been visiting him at visiting hours.

I hadn't heard anything new from Surreya in five weeks. We were going to Uncle's house the next afternoon and I was going to call her from there. The whole family would sleep over at Uncle's except Stepmother, who would be alone and resting.

No adults were home this afternoon. I asked my cousin to babysit the toddlers for a while playing in the yard while I made a call.

"Hey, it's Surreya."

"Hey, it's me, how are you? It feels so long since I heard from you."

"Thanks, Shemal gyan, I'm fine. What about you?"

"Okay, tired, working day and night! My stepmother has got another boy."

"Poor you! Well, I've met Mahnaz again. We have planned to start studying! I can tell you more when we meet."

"I have laundry day tomorrow in the same place. Can you come and help me with the laundry?"

"Yes, that's fine. I can bring some tea and homemade cakes and come at two o'clock. Is that okay?"

"Yes, that'll be fine. See you tomorrow."

I wondered what Surreya meant by her and Mahnaz having

plans to start studying. How dangerous would it be for them? I knew it wasn't about education. They were not allowed to go to school because they were married, neither for the system nor for their husbands. It had to be something against the regime or against Khalkhali, but it could be deadly. I couldn't help but speculate about the different interpretations of what Surreya had said.

I carried all the laundry, hot water and everything I needed to the creek that was behind the house. I asked my stepmother not to send the children to me for the whole afternoon. I needed to be at peace with all the laundry I needed to take care of.

Surreya appeared just at two p.m. She took off her long coat and shawl, found a rock to sit on, and began to help me with the laundry while we talked.

"I called Reza and asked to see Mahnaz again. He got a little pensive at first and asked why. But I said I don't have any friends that I can meet sometimes. Mahnaz and I are in the same situation, and we can understand each other. We can be friends and talk to each other. He said he'd arrange it on one condition. That I never reveal what relationship he and I have. I have to say I'm his wife number two. I promised to do so.

"He called my father-in-law in the evening and said that I could have a day with Sirwan again.

"The next day, my father-in-law drove me to Orumiyeh. There Reza met me as usual and after a few hours he drove me to Mahnaz. On the way there, Reza told me that he had informed Ayatollah Khalkhali that he also had a siga wife, and that no one knew about it. Khalkhali had let me meet his wife, Mahnaz. He had told Reza that he had to take responsibility for ensuring that we, Mahnaz and I, would not do any nonsense or reveal what was going on."

"How stupid both Reza and Khalkhali must be to believe it!"

"The older lady who recognized me opened the door. Mahnaz was more alert this time. She was very happy to see me. We sat down in the living room and had coffee. The lady kept praying for almost an hour and then she would shower and wash her hair. We had time to talk, but Mahnaz was afraid that our voices could be recorded. We chose to write on a sheet of paper instead. At the same time, we pretended to be talking about God, prayers, Ramadan and fasting in Farsi. Mahnaz wrote that she could not go on living like this. She intended to poison Khalkhali first, and then escape from there.

"She wrote: *he smokes lots of tiriac every night and also forces me to smoke with him. Then he becomes like crazy and rapes me several times a night.*

"She hated herself and her mother for agreeing to subject her to this. I reminded her that it was for her father's life. He could be executed if she put her plan into action. She cried and said that her father would rather choose to die than see his daughter as a sex slave of a mullah. She showed me lots of bruises on her body. He slapped her during the sex act. Then he got more excited, she said."

"What did you say about wanting to study? What are your plans?"

"Mahnaz wanted to know about my story, and I told her what a pig Reza is and that I am his sex slave to save the life of my husband. We plan for me to contact the peshmerga secretly and tell them about my and Mahnaz's situation. We want them to help us take revenge against the regime and Khalkhali before we flee to the border areas.

"Both Mahnaz and I are sure that once these idiots have had enough of us, they will kill us. They will surely kill Sirwan and

Mahnaz's father too. We'd better get revenge before they kill us."

"Surreya, it's such a dangerous thought! You are inexperienced young girls and will be exposed before you succeed with your plan. How could you get into contact with the peshmerga with the difficult situation that prevails in the city?"

"I am corresponding with Sirwan's brothers who are peshmerga and intend to write to them about me and Mahnaz. They will help us."

"I am so scared and concerned for you and do not want to see or hear that you have been injured or imprisoned."

"We have no choice, my friend. We die inside every time we are subjected to their rapes." The silence that followed reinforced the horror of what had just been said. Despairingly, I cried silently, but Surreya was calm and collected. She seemed to have made her decision and I couldn't or didn't want to stop her.

***

It had now been a couple of months since my stepmother gave birth. She hadn't visited Dad in all that time, but today Uncle drove her to Orumiyeh for them to visit him together.

Again, a new list was read on the radio of twelve Kurdish prisoners executed on Khalkhali's orders in the prison in Orumiyeh. My father's name thankfully wasn't on the list this time either!

When they got home, I immediately saw from Uncle that something serious had happened. He was sad and saggy.

"What's happened? Have you heard anything about Dad, Uncle?"

"No, not about Dad, but about the older couple we helped last time. Their daughter Kajal was among those executed yesterday. I met her father outside the prison. He was completely despondent and devastated. They have requested a large sum of money from him to hand over his daughter's body. He walked around among people begging for money. He cried and prayed that we would help them pay to have their daughter's body buried in their home village of Qalatan." Uncle cried as he recounted the story.

I was so sad and upset and saw her mother in front of me. How would this old, wrinkled, sad mother cope with this?

I asked Uncle if we could go to Qalatan to meet the old couple and support them with money and other things. He thought it was a good idea and he bought some groceries like rice, oil and wheat flour to bring to them.

My bonus grandfather who is a kind man also wanted to contribute something, and also talked to my uncle and other relatives. We collected ten thousand tuman, as well as a lot of groceries. Uncle and I would go there the next day. It was hard to sleep at night, as soon as I closed my eyes, Kajal's hanged body was in front of me, and I wanted to scream so that everyone heard: I hated this fanatical mullah regime... I hated them!

At seven o'clock in the morning we were on our way to Qalatan.

In the village of Qalatan, we were looking for the old couple's home. In front of a door, a few people were gathered. We asked them for the grieving old couple. They showed us the house where they lived. We walked in through a small yard without any greenery, with chicken coops and an outhouse. A younger woman met us and led us in. In the room, Kajal's father sat alone in one corner and in the other corner her old mother with two other women. A photo of Kajal hung on the wall, a beautiful innocent young girl with enormously sad eyes.

I walked up to Kajal's mother and hugged her. She didn't cry but her body was shivering. She just repeated: my Kajal, my Kajal... I cried inconsolable in her arms. It was so heartbreaking, when it was heard how Kajal's father and also Uncle cried. He was old, sad and despondent but dared not say more than that Kajal was innocent. She was young. She had dreams...

We left everything we had with us to the old, devastated man. He prayed that no parents would ever have to feel this sadness. I promised Kajal's mother to return soon again.

On our way home, we were sad, silent, and pensive. I saw the horrible picture of how they had tortured her before they had hanged her. The anger and hatred of everyone in the fanatical inhuman mullah regime consumed me and I felt that I had to do something, actively resist them. The guilt of seeing, of knowing the suffering of so many victims, while I sat quietly and did not act against the regime weighed on me.

Unlike my everyday ritual, waking up early in the morning, fixing breakfast, cleaning afterwards, sewing and doing laundry, I had had to sleep a few extra hours on this day. I was awake until five o'clock in the morning and finished sewing some garments to be delivered before the evening. When I woke up, I didn't see anyone in the room. I wondered where everyone, siblings and stepmothers, had gone. I went to my grandfather's house who lived next door to us and saw that everyone was there. Grandpa's wife had invited them to breakfast. She was so kind and caring. She immediately got up and fetched my portion of breakfast with both fried eggs, fresh baked bread, cheese, and tea. I was enjoying the food when Grandpa came in. We got up to show him respect according to our Kurdish culture. He said:

"Shemal, I want to talk to you alone when you've finished eating your breakfast."

"Okay, bapire."

I finished my breakfast quickly and went to the next room where Grandpa was.

"My daughter, that family in Qalatan whose daughter was murdered by the regime, can you and I visit them in a few days?"

"Yes, bapire, Uncle and I were there yesterday. What's on your mind?"

"I have some money of my own that I want to leave to them. I also want to meet them to comfort them and show that we exist and grieve with them. What is happening in our area is everyone's fate. We must stick together and grieve together. We must help each other so that our enemy does not succeed in wiping us out."

I was so impressed by Grandpa's wise words. He was almost a hundred years old and had experienced so much in his life. He recalled our old historical events with Qazi Mohammad and the independent year with the Mahabad Republic in 1945. Normally he was very quiet and introverted, but he and I had always had a good relationship. He had said he trusted me as a wise person. I promised to take him with me to Qalatan whenever he wanted. He gave me twenty tuman and wanted me to spend them only for my own needs, not for my siblings' ones, and I promised to do that.

Three days after my visit to Qalatan, I was called home to my uncle because he wanted to talk to me. His son picked me up.

When I stepped into my uncle's living room, he was with a man and woman unknown to me. I greeted them and sat down near the woman.

Uncle said, "Shemal, these people have a message and letter for you. Do you know them?"

I got a little scared and replied politely.

"Unfortunately, not, but I'd be grateful if they'd tell me where they're from and what kind of letter and message they have for me."

Uncle looked around to see that no doors or windows were open. No other could hear us!

"Shemal, I know you're in touch with your father's party and the peshmerga. Do not be afraid and trust me. I am also a party comrade and a friend of peshmerga. These are from Sardasht and are our party friends. In the future, they will be our contacts with the party and the peshmerga. I want you not to trust anyone else."

I relaxed and felt a tremendous sense of security. I had absolutely no idea that my uncle could be a party sympathizer and activist.

"Oh, how glad I'll be, Uncle, that you support me and our party. Can I get the letter and hear what the message is?"

The lady introduced herself as Zara and handed me an envelope.

The man's name was Qadir and was the physical bond between me, Uncle and peshmerga. He wanted me to do some administrative work to get more supporters of the party, who could be helpful when peshmerga forces would carry out their military attacks on regime stations around the city. It was important that the peshmerga's struggle was reinforced from within cities, he said.

"But don't forget, never trust anyone before you ask us about the person who wants to cooperate!"

"Yes, I'll be careful. But how can I contact you if necessary?"

"We come here to your uncle once a month. Then we have all the information about the assignments that you are going to perform and be a part of. Your uncle is our safest contact in the city."

We talked and had coffee for a while. Uncle reminded me that:

"Remember, my family and my sister don't know anything about this. So, when you get home, don't tell them about these people or our meeting. You can say that I needed your help with a banking case and writing letters to the bank. I want you to read the letter you received here, and we'll burn it before you go home. You can go to another room if you want to read it alone."

I chose to read the letter there with them.

We welcome you to our party as a credible comrade. We will trust you and give you important assignments once a month in the future. Never save the letters you receive from us. You and your uncle will be our strategic contacts in Khaneh. Being able to find safe routes and contacts for the activity of peshmerga in the city is the first and most important mission you have. Always reason with your uncle if you become unsure. We are in constant contact with him. Your friends at PDKI

I looked tearfully at my uncle who saw that I was about to start crying. He got up and came close to me, hugged me.

"I know you're crying from the loss of your father. But I'm here for you forever. I love you as my own child and I am proud of you as a brave young party comrade. We do our best to help with the struggle of our peshmergas. We don't give up."

I burned the letter and said goodbye to our friends. My uncle's son drove me home.

My stepmother was very curious as to why my uncle had called me home to him.

I replied that he needed help with banking and things like that. She bought it with a hesitant look but asked nothing more.

***

All night I sat awake, pondering which of the friends I had would be reliable enough to involve in our party supporters' chain. Surreya was not suitable because her husband, Sirwan, and his brothers were Komala. It is the left wing of the peshmerga. Komala and PDKI did not cooperate. They competed with each other as political counter-partners. I came across a woman who had come and baked bread for us all these years. Her two sons were peshmerga at PDKI. Yes, I could contact her. She knew everyone in the city and knew everything about everyone. I had to think about how I could meet her and talk to her gently about it.

A week later, by spending the night at my uncle's home, I managed to plan the meeting with the baker. Uncle told his sister he needed my help with some paperwork. Late in the afternoon we took a taxi that stopped in front of the door of the baker. Uncle left me and we agreed that he would pick me up in an hour.

Nervously, I rang the doorbell.

A younger woman opened the door.

"Hey, is Hajar khanum home?"

"Yes, go ahead." She called out for her.

Hajar came out and asked the younger woman to go in to her child.

She recognized me and invited me in.

"How nice that you have the way past," she said.

"But do you have a lot of people with you right now?"

"No, it's just my daughter-in-law with her child. We can sit in another room to ourselves."

I was a little puzzled that she knew why I was here? Could I trust her? How could I know that she was not cooperating with the regime?

We entered a room she called the guest room. It was two rooms away from the room where the daughter-in-law was.

"How are you, Hajar khanum?"

"I feel good compared to many others. What about your father? I am so sorry for everything that has happened to him and your family. May God punish these mullahs who have ruined things for all of us. So much better lives we had before they came."

"Do you think the Shah's regime was better than this?"

"Yes, my daughter, it was. But I was never as happy as when the peshmerga were in the city and everything was under the control of the Kurds."

"Which peshmerga group did you think was the best? PDKI or Komala?"

"My daughter, I have all my heart, brain and blood for PDKI. I have two brothers, three cousins and my sons who are peshmerga with them. I love your father who was the father of all peshmerga. May these mullahs go to hell. What can I do for you, my daughter?"

"Can I trust you?"

"I can swear by the Koran if you want. I swear on the lives of my brothers and sons that you can trust me in everything."

"Do you have any contact with peshmerga?"

"Not really, but I bake bread and send them through some that I trust. I've been able to see my sons twice since they fled to the mountains. Why?"

"I need your help to find those who sympathize with PDKI and peshmerga and want to actively resist the regime. I have to be one hundred percent sure that they are against the regime and want to help with missions."

"I guessed there was an important reason when you came here. You can trust me. I know everyone in the city. I know who's doing what. But you are young, why are you risking your life? Isn't it enough that your father is in prison and your grandmother died of grief?"

"That and much more is what makes me feel that I can't accept what the regime is doing to us Kurds. If we don't stick together against the regime, they will take everything away from us. You see how they execute tens of Kurds daily in Orumiyeh. We must strengthen the power of the peshmerga in the city. We have to help each other."

"What do you want me to do? I'll do what you tell me."

"Find several real peshmerga sympathizers to form a group that can take on active missions. You meet many. Talk discreetly with those you know you can trust. Never mention my name. You can, when you're sure, send the people's names to me."

"Okay, I already know a few who think the way you do. But I need to talk to them before I can mention them to you. How can I reach you?"

"You know my stepmother and you know where we live now. You can come by and pretend you just want to visit. Our code for the friends you find can become bread. If you find any friends who want to be connected to the group, you can have two or three loaves of bread to give away. I need to have some who are really opposed to the regime that we can rely on to give missions."

"I'll work on it and get back to you. Do not be in a hurry and do not trust anyone. You are young and hurt, but you have to be very careful, or you risk your life. I know many here in the city and will take safe steps. I, like you, hate this regime and their pasdar. But I'm not going to end up in their prison or have to leave my home for the mountains. I'll come by when I have something to tell."

Uncle was waiting for me when I left Hajar's house. We went to his house, and I told him what happened at Hajar's.

"She was very kind and positive about working with us, but she is very scared and wants to be careful and discreet in what she does. We have a plan that she will come by ours when she has any news."

"It sounds good, you should also be careful about yourself and not act solely with emotions. You must be professional and discreet."

***

We learned on this day that my father's sentence was fixed at twenty years in prison. We celebrated it and were happy that he wouldn't be executed. The letter from Ayatollah Montazeri to Ayatollah Khalkhali was delivered by my uncle. He got to meet Khalkhali in person and, in addition to the letter, he also had to pay him a large sum of money. But it felt good even though we had gotten rid of everything we owned and lived like a poor family. Dad got to live and the hope that he could be free one day was our joy.

I continued to sew and embroider for people to earn food money for everyday life. Thank God I received an order to sew an entire set of bedding that would also be embroidered for someone who would be married a month later. The mother of the bride came to us and introduced herself as Amine. She said she had four daughters and a son who was seventeen. She had been a widow for five years. They were from Bokan but moved to our town of Khaneh three years ago. I didn't know about them before, but she claimed to have known about my father and our family for a long time. She was a very kind and motherly woman in her forties. On the very first visit, she asked if she could invite me to her house so that I could get to know her daughters and befriend them.

Two weeks later, she came with two of her daughters and wanted me to also sew their Kurdish dresses for her sister's wedding. She had a lot of homemade cakes with her and handed them to me, really trying to attract me to herself and her home! She even approached my stepmother and invited her to her house! The daughters were eleven and thirteen years old, sweet, slightly shy girls who said nothing. They did as their mother said. The big sister who was going to get married was nineteen years old and was not there. Amine persuaded me to agree to visit them the following week when I had finished sewing part of the order. Then I was also invited to lunch.

I asked Stepmother what she thought of Amine and her way of being. She replied that Amine was nice, and I could well befriend her daughters. But it didn't feel quite right to me! I've always had a bit of a hard time trusting people I didn't get to know properly. At least I promised to visit them. It had been a week since Amine was with us. Their entire order was complete except for the daughters' dresses, and I would visit them during the day. I felt a little fear and discomfort inside of seeing her again, but I went there anyway.

A taxi drove me, as they lived a bit outside the city. Once there, the door was open.

I cautiously walked in through a tapered path towards a small farm. In the yard I saw a small tomato and vegetable patch, a large cherry tree and two smaller vine trees stretching over the wall of the house. Amine met me at the entrance, hugged me and welcomed me into a well-decorated living room and a large kitchen with dining area. It reminded me of our nice house and kitchen before the regime took it away from us.

I asked where the daughters were, and she told me they were out in the bazaar and would be coming home soon! There were some pictures on the walls, including a picture of a young boy with a man. The boy was so similar to her that there was no mistaking the fact that it was her son.

"Is it your son with his father?"

"Yes, it is. He was seven years old in this picture and his father passed away a year later after a severe illness. I've been single with all four kids and worked hard to support them."

"Sorry! What are you working as?"

She sighed deeply and replied.

"I was the school principal for many years, but after the revolution I was not approved by the regime to stay. We had some land and orchards that I have sold and lived on. And I've had some small jobs as a private secretary and written various documents for private companies for periods. Through several relatives living in the big cities like Tehran and Tabriz, I have good connections with big businessmen there. I knew your father from before through my business contacts. He was a good-looking man and I wished I could have flirted with him sometimes, but he showed no interest in me then, hehe…" She laughed.

"Oh, you know my father from before. But how did you come to move here? Do you have relatives here in Khaneh?"

"No, to make a long story short. I was forced to move with my daughters and son after the regime took over our city. My son was young and missed his father. He became directly involved in the illegal political resistance movement. To protect him, I had to move to an unknown city and live anonymously. But unfortunately, my son didn't stop his stupidities, so he was arrested by the regime five months ago. He is imprisoned in the same prison in Orumiyeh as your father."

"How sad to hear. Hope he's doing well and can get out soon. Who will your eldest daughter marry?"

"She's marrying a man from Maraga who works as an official in the pasdar Group!"

I felt a pain in my stomach and my pulse increased instantly. I was shocked and scared that this was a trap for me. I decided to leave the stuff and get out of there. She walked towards the fridge to get me a glass of cold drink. I left the clothes on the table in the kitchen.

"I'm sorry to have to go now, my siblings are alone."

"But I thought you'd eat with us?"

"I'm actually fasting today. Thank you, anyway, greet your daughters. The dresses will be ready in a couple of days so you can come and get them then. Goodbye!"

She came up to me, held my arm, and said:

"But wait a minute, you accepted to be our lunch guest. Then why do you come here fasting? What's the fool's play?"

"No, I said I'll come by with the stuff and I'd be happy to greet your daughters. But now they're not home and I'm fasting, so it'll have to be another time. Like I said I have to go home!"

"But it was boring, I've cooked special food for you to come. Promise you'll come another time. I'll come over to you in a couple of days. Goodbye and greet your mother."

I almost ran out of her house and took the first taxi that passed by home to my uncle. I have to tell him about this woman. The fear made me almost shake.

***

The taxi stopped at Uncle's house. He sat in the shade of a tree and smoked.

"Hey, Shemal, what a surprise that you show up at this time."

"Khala, Uncle, are you alone or..."

"Yes, I am by myself, the others are with my wife's mother. What has happened? You seem to be stressed."

"Yes, I was very intimidated. I am both hungry and thirsty. Can we go to the kitchen?"

We went into the kitchen and found some leftovers from the day before that I could heat up. I drank a couple of glasses of water, and told my uncle what had happened, and about Amine. He became worried and thought I should leave the city immediately, until he could check who she was and who she worked for.

"But you can't do that, you know my siblings live on my work and I take care of them all the time. How will they cope?"

"I'll help them with the money. Your uncle in Shno will also help. They have their mother, and your sister Nasrin is big enough to help her mother. I don't want you to stay here until I find out what she's after."

We went to our house. There I quickly packed my clothes and my sewing machine with accessories. Uncle drove me straight to Mahabad for me to disappear for a while. My biological mother lived there with her family. But Uncle didn't think I should live with her.

"There is a great risk that the regime through this woman will find you with your mother."

I had to stay with an acquaintance of my uncle's wife in

Mahabad. Uncle assured me that he knew them well and that it was safe for me to be there for a few days. He would contact me when he learned more about the woman. I finished sewing the dresses of Amine's daughters that evening, so that my uncle would take them to my stepmother. She would have to hand them over to Amine. Uncle said he would talk to his sister and explain the situation.

"She's not allowed to tell Amine where you are. She also has to lie to the children about you being in Tehran. I will even inform your uncle in Shno."

It was a turbulent time in my life again. The uncertainty worried me. How would my siblings cope? Who would inform Surreya of my escape now? I had been ordered by my uncle not to go out, not to call anyone and not to answer the phone where I was.

A smaller room, a walk-in closet with no windows that the family had emptied, became my bedroom. It was behind the couple's own room. The man in the house had also dug a hole under the floor, in the middle of the room, where I could hide if necessary.

The woman in the house was well instructed to not leave the front door open. She wasn't allowed to let anyone in she didn't know. She would never confirm that she knew me or had seen me. The children in the family were small and did not understand why I was with them. I had also been instructed that if the doorbell rang, I would sit in my small room and lock the door. Listen to what was heard from the outside. If she spoke loudly, and said that she knew no such man, I would go down the hole and pull the lid over me. On top of the hole was a thick hand-woven carpet that covered the entire floor.

My host family was very kind and caring. After a week, I

hadn't heard anything from anyone. I had not dared to go outside the house, as it was full of regime militias and even djash everywhere in Mahabad. But I had sewn both clothes and curtains for my host family.

It was seven o'clock in the evening when the man in my host family came home from his job and handed me a closed envelope from my uncle. I opened it and read at once.

She is the regime's spy and in search of you. She's been to get her sewn clothes and paid big to your stepmother. I'll come over tomorrow to drive you to Tehran. Be prepared. Khala

I cried and panicked knowing that I was in the spotlight for the regime and had to live secretly. "How am I going to cope with not seeing my father in prison, my siblings, my contacts to the party, Hajar, Surreya...?"

The host family gave me comfort and a lot of support and assured me that it will work out.

"There are several of us around you who will help in the best way."

It was hard to sleep at night and I cried a lot. The loss of my siblings, my father and Surreya was very great. I first decided to tell my uncle about Surreya and ask him to help us stay in touch. He would understand her. But then I changed my mind. What if she didn't want me to tell my uncle about her? But how would I ask my uncle to help us with the contact? Surreya would be disappointed and perhaps frightened if she didn't hear from me. Oh God, why did this have to be so hard? No, I refuse to go to Tehran. All these thoughts stole the night's sleep from me.

My uncle came to Mahabad. He told me that Amine was the regime's agent and spy. The peshmerga knew her. But they did not hurt her due to the fact that her son was a political prisoner. She had become a spy to save her son from execution. It was an agreement the regime had with her. As long as she cooperated with them, her son would live. Her daughter had married one of pasdar's principals and was also cooperating with the regime. Amine had received warnings from the peshmerga several times, but she kept spying because she had no choice. Her only son's life was in danger. She was also a victim of the regime, though in a different way.

Uncle told me that she had been to our house and asked where I was and when I would come home. My stepmother had told her that I had traveled to Tehran to find a job. My uncle had consulted with my uncle in Shno, and they had decided that I would stay hidden in Mahabad for a while longer. That's where I stayed until we found a better solution. It was nice not to have to move to Tehran. I wasn't allowed to be seen and couldn't call anyone. My uncle had asked my host family to make sure that happened. He promised that he would keep me updated by occasionally coming to visit or sending letters.

***

It had been a whole month since I started living in hiding in Mahabad. Hiding meant being inside all the time. In addition to helping with the housework, I sewed some, wrote my diary every night, and helped the wife of the house learn to read and write. She had four children and was only thirty years old. Since she had never been to school, she was illiterate, but she was very talented and easy to teach. She could draw amazingly fine birds, which was her interest. She quickly learned to both read and write. They were still very kind to me and hadn't got tired of me living with them.

My uncle in Shno had sent letters through my uncle in

Khaneh, saying that he had been visiting my father. Dad wanted to see me on his next visit. Uncle promised to come and fetch me from Mahabad to Orumiyeh. How happy I was to be able to visit my dad. I must try and sew him nice, warm pajamas before then. I had the money I had received from my bonus grandfather left. I asked the man in the house to buy fabric and lining materials. I prayed my God that I would meet Surreya outside the prison. Hoping she would be there; I wrote her a letter.

The joy and anticipation of meeting both Dad and maybe Surreya made me count the days and have a hope to live for. In the short letter I wrote.

Hi Surreya, sorry I haven't been able to get in touch and just disappeared! I was forced to. It's a spy who seems to have been tasked with following me and dragging me into something fishy. My uncle knows about it. You can trust him. I haven't told him anything about you. I miss you and think every day about you and also about your friend M. Hugs, S

***

Two weeks later, my uncle arrived in Mahabad early one morning. After breakfast, we drove together to Orumiyeh. Uncle begged me not to walk around as we waited outside the prison. He wanted me to try not to be seen so much because there could be spies among the waiting. I promised to do as he said.

We were now out of prison again. Lots of people stood and waited. I was standing next to my uncle in a corner, but my eyes were looking for a young woman who wore a colorful shawl on her head and was made up. I found one in the crowd. Without saying anything to Uncle, I walked towards her, she stood a hundred yards away from us. She stood with her back to us and didn't see me. When I arrived, I spontaneously grabbed her arm. She turned around and I saw it was Surreya. We hugged each other. I left the letter in her hand and said:

"Read it before you go in. Don't bring the letter in!"

I left her and quickly went back to my uncle who was really angry with me.

"We had an agreement, didn't we? Who is she? Why did you run away? Don't you realize you're in danger?"

I was silent and looked away. He didn't give up and wanted to know who the woman I went to was.

"She's the sister of a friend of mine."

"Or the sister of some boy you're in love with?"

"No, Uncle, nothing like that. It's a close friend I've missed so much."

We waited half an hour. I knew where Surreya stood. The speakers began to sound, names were shouted for the prisoners who had visiting hours. A wave of worry and stress went through the crowd. Everyone wanted to come forward. Some armed pasdar standing outside the entrance yelled at people to go back and wait. I saw that Surreya was coming towards us. I was frightened, shaking and had palpitations. She came over and greeted my uncle. She was standing so close to me, and I felt her hand go into my coat pocket and out quickly again. She talked about how she and her family knew my father and they all prayed for his life. Uncle did not recognize her but thanked. She quickly left us and went back to her seat. I put my hand in my coat pocket and felt a rolled-up piece of paper. I almost felt sick with fear.

We heard them calling my dad's name. As I followed Uncle towards the entrance, I looked around among the crowd. I didn't see Surreya, and I knew Reza had picked her up.

We passed the same dark corridors as before until we entered the meeting point, the long wall with windows of thick glass separating outside from inside. We were referred by the prison guard to stand at window number three.

Dad came walking by himself without support this time. We picked up the phone at the same time.

"Hey, Dad, how are you?"

He had the same knitwear on as last time. His voice trembled and I could see that his tears were flowing.

"Hello, my beloved Shemal, how are you?"

"I'm fine, Dad, why are you crying?"

"I dream such worried dreams about you. I'm worried about you."

"I'm healthy and I'm fine, Dad. My siblings are doing well, too. Don't be alarmed. We'll be fine."

Dad cried so he couldn't talk. I know something had happened in there with him. He was strong and would not give up. Uncle took over the phone. Both Dad and I cried, looking at each other through the thick glass, the wall that separated us.

"Ahmad what is it, why are you so emotionally charged? It's fine with everyone. Everything is going well. The fruits on the garden begin to ripen. Do not be alarmed, everything will work out."

Uncle was talking on, and Dad's gaze with tears in his eyes only saw me. I shuddered at the thought that it might be the last time I saw him. Is that what he knew and cried for? Had he been told they were going to execute him? Had he been told I was at risk of being arrested? There was no conversation between Uncle and Dad. Time ran out and the phone went silent. Uncle put the phone back and turned to the prison guard standing behind us.

"Why was our conversation closed down? I didn't have time to hear my brother's voice before the phone went silent."

"Your time is only five minutes and it's fast."

We had no choice. Dad had already left the meeting place without waving goodbye. I didn't see if it was some guard pulling him away or if he went by himself.

We were directed towards the exit by the prison guard and followed him out.

Out there, I looked around to see if I could see any familiar face, but Uncle took quick steps toward the car. We drove in heavy silence all the way towards Mahabad.

Uncle drove on to Shno's home after I had been dropped off with the same host family I had been staying with for over a month now.

I quickly went into the bathroom and closed the door. I picked out the rolled-up letter that Surreya had stuffed into my coat pocket. She had written on the back of my letter to her.

Guessed you had to disappear underground. I've missed you. I will talk to your uncle and ask him to help us have contact. Some things have happened to me and my thirteen-year-old friend. Take care. Hugs, S.

***

Although the family I lived with was very kind and respected me, I felt like a prisoner. I still wasn't allowed to go out or call anyone. It had been ten days since the visit to Dad. Nightmares about both my dad and me meant that I couldn't sleep much at night. One night I woke up dreaming that I was tied to a tree and had a black sack pulled down over my head that covered my eyes. They shot me and just as I felt myself falling to die, I woke up from sleep feeling how sweaty my whole body was. For the rest of the night, I sat awake feeling sick and crying.

This day was Friday and the man in my host family was free. He told us to prepare food, tea and fruit to drive out of the city to a mountainous area to have a family picnic. I was really looking forward to it. I felt like my lungs were hungry for a pinch of fresh air.

He drove the wife, the children and me, in his Peykan. After an hour's journey, we stopped next to a roaring river where it was green with trees and bushes. We chose a corner behind the trees where we were not visible from the road. We set the table for a light coffee break before lunch two hours later. He told us that we would soon have two guests visiting!

"What! Who are they?" I asked in surprise.

"It's your uncle with a friend of yours."

"Wow, does Uncle know we're here?"

"Yes, we have agreed on this place."

I turned to the wife and asked her.

"Did you know about this?"

"Yes, but my husband asked me not to tell you before."

I was so happy that I began to cry with joy, guessing that it was Surreya he had with him.

Twenty minutes later, Uncle arrived with Surreya in a pickup truck.

Surreya and I hugged and cried together for a while. Uncle pulled me from her, hugged me, and said:

"I've also missed you and have good news for you."

"What, Uncle? Say it!"

"We can have a coffee first and then we can walk and talk. One more thing, before I forget, is that your uncle and I have judged that it is best for all of you to move to Shno and live there. Still, it is your uncle who has the main responsibility for all of you. Your father has wished for that and asked him for it. It is not far between Shno and Khaneh. I can come by you very often and make sure you and Surreya can have the opportunity to meet as well."

"I also think it will be safer for us that you and your family live in Shno. No one knows me in Shno," Surreya said.

"But we don't have a place to live in Shno."

"All of us in the family have helped each other and bought you a smaller home. It's much bigger and better compared to where you live now."

I felt like I was a little shocked by so many new events and so much information. I fell silent until Surreya tugged at me and said:

"What is it? Why are you so quiet? It'll be fine. We have Uncle with us as support."

"I'll leave you alone now so you can talk alone. Now I go back to the others. You can also get there when you're done with your girl talk hehe…"

He left us. We sat down on a rock, the sun warmed, and the sound of the running water was like a soothing melody.

"Surreya, I feel so bad. I have nightmares every night about either me or my dad getting executed. I have felt like a prisoner these months in Mahabad."

I started crying like a disconsolate child. Surreya came closer and hugged me and kissed me comfortingly on the hair.

"I understand you, friend, but we're all living in a nightmare right now. Sirwan told me that at least once a week they subject all the prisoners to mock executions as a method of torture. He fainted the last time when they exposed him to it. We must be strong and not let these animals win over us."

"How did you get in touch with my uncle? What have you

told him?"

"I went to his shop one day, and luckily he was alone there. After introducing myself, I told him the full story of my husband's arrest, and my vulnerability for saving his life. About how you and I met and about Mahnaz's situation. I immediately felt safe with him. He is so fatherly and has been wonderful and helpful. I trust him as I do my own father. His secret contact with the peshmerga could, in the event of an emergency, save both you and me."

"Did you know about Amine and her daughters?"

"Yes, but I never got in touch with her. My mother-in-law had at one point run into her. Then the mother-in-law's sister did some research on her. Amine is from Bokan and moved to Khaneh to work as a spy for pasdar and the regime. Her eldest daughter married one of the great heads of the regime's militias, the pasdar, and she is also a spy. But now she and her children have moved from Khaneh. Many believe that they have moved to Tabriz because her daughter's husband has been given a higher position there. Unfortunately, she managed to expose two young guys, who are in prison now. Thanks to your uncle, you were saved from her plans."

"What about Mahnaz? Have you met?"

"Yes, we have. Last time she was at her mother's house in Mahabad, we got to meet at her aunt's house who is reliable. Khalkhali seems to have grown tired of her because she does not function as a human being unless she is under the influence of opium. She transforms into a rigid doll which he dislikes. Her threshold for opium has increased so he can't fix it. She is afraid that he will make sure that she is murdered or disappears."

"Ugh! How hard. But what are the plans before something terrible happens?"

"She's going to poison him and the lady in the house and then run away. That it can cost both her and her father's life, she is aware of, but wants to do it anyway. Vulnerability consumes her."

"How are you doing with Reza?"

"He's just a pig and has another sex slave now. He's not that interested in me any more. But he continues to plan my dates and overnight stays with Sirwan because my father-in-law gives him so much money and gifts every time. I'm trying to find a way out so Sirwan and I can escape during the night when we're alone. I have written to Sirwan's brothers who know the situation. I'm waiting for them to direct me a little bit in the plans."

"Oh, my God, Surreya. You and Mahnaz are really playing with fire. You will be exposed before you can do anything. You know there are a lot of spies everywhere."

"Yes, we know it's playing with death. But the life we have now is also to play with death. Both Mahnaz and I know that soon, when these idiots get tired of us, they will make sure we disappear. Our captive men they will surely murder too. Many more women who have been victimized like us, have finally disappeared without a trace."

"But how will you be able to meet or have contact with Mahnaz in the future?"

"Her aunt is like your uncle. Mahnaz trusts her. Every time she is with her mother, once a month, we meet at her aunt's house who calls me in advance when she knows Mahnaz is coming. I will take a taxi to Mahabad. My in-laws are kind and trust me. They don't ask much. I get enough money from them so I can do it. Mahnaz's aunt is also like your uncle in contact with the peshmerga and hates the regime and pasdar. She's very helpful.

"With the help of your uncle, I will find a solution to how

we can keep in touch when you live in Shno. Don't be alarmed. Now let's go back to the others."

It smelled like dolma from afar. We ate, drank tea and hung out for a few hours before it was time for Uncle and Surreya to drive home to Khaneh. I was saddened and cried when we hugged goodbye, but Uncle comforted me that he would come and pick me up in two weeks. Something to look forward to.

***

I finished sewing the garments I had started for my host family and then cleaned the whole house for her as thanks for allowing me to stay with them for over two months.

My uncle showed up one early afternoon to pick me up for Shno. He told me that he and my uncle decided together that it was safer for me that I didn't move back home to Khaneh. I was able to stay with my uncle for a week until my family moved to Shno. The packing was almost done, an hour later I was ready to come along. But Uncle suggested that we first visit my biological mother who lived in Mahabad. I hadn't seen her in more than a year.

We made a short visit. On the way, we had decided not to tell her about my situation, but just to say that we had driven past Mahabad and took the opportunity to meet her. My uncle had good contact with my mother's husband and family for a few years. They had great respect for him. Mom asked about how my dad was doing in prison and how me and my siblings were doing.

I gave her a brief description that everyone was fine even though the situation was as heavy and boring as it was. Unfortunately, I did not have a close mother-daughter relationship with my mother, as she left me before I was two years old. The loss of a mother's love I had replaced throughout my childhood with my grandmother's love and presence as the mother in my life. My dad was so actively present and supportive throughout my life that I was pretty happy with what I had.

After we'd met, we drove towards Shno, which is about a hundred kilometers from Mahabad. I was looking forward to meeting my cousin Saadat who was almost the same age as me. We loved each other and had a very close relationship. We could tell each other everything. However, I hadn't told her about my political involvement, because her mother wasn't someone I could trust. She was very conservative, and I knew she could get Saadat to tell her everything.

A happy evening with food with my uncle's family ended with me sharing a bedroom with my cousin Saadat, but her mother thought that Saadat's little sister should also sleep with us. All three lay on mattresses on the floor. When little sister had fallen asleep, we talked until dawn. Saadat was happily in love with a guy and told me so much about it that she didn't even ask how I had been doing and why I had been in Mahabad for so long. But I was glad she didn't ask because then I didn't have to lie to her.

The next day Uncle showed me the house they had bought for us. It was barely five hundred yards from theirs. A moderately sized newly built house with a smaller garden. The house wasn't fully built yet, but ready enough to live in and more comfortable than where we lived. I counted the days until next week when my entire family, and our household goods, would be moved to Shno.

I asked my uncle about our finances, "What assets do we have to live on?"

"Your father had some money with a business partner in

Tehran who managed it. I get a sum every quarter and that's what you must live on."

It felt good that we could live on Dad's money instead of the family's. My dad had always been the one who helped both the family and other needy people financially and with other things. It felt so heavy to see my family in such a tight financial situation that the relatives needed to help us.

***

My siblings and stepmother arrived in Shno a week later. We furnished two rooms and the kitchen in the new house. There was electricity, a refrigerator, a real bathroom, an outhouse, hot and cold water and a heating element in the house so we did not have to have an oil stove for heating in the winter. The oil stoves smelled so bad that you woke up with a headache every winter morning. Now I could sit in another room and sew at night when the others slept in the big room and no longer had to sit under an oil lamp and sew.

Shoresh, my soon-to-be three-year-old little brother saw me as his mother before I had to disappear from him. When they arrived in my uncle's car a few days earlier, I ran up to him to hug and kiss him. But he showed that he was angry with me, turned around and walked away from me. Nasrin told me that the first few nights without me he had found it very difficult to eat and sleep. He had cried and called for me. Nasrin said Shoresh had fallen asleep with one of my garments or my shoe in his arms. I was so moved that I cried. But after a while, Shoresh himself came up to me again, not wanting to leave me for a second. God, how we had missed each other. All my siblings were so depressed by everything that had happened and was happening in their lives. In the evenings I saw how, when they were going to sleep, they crawled close to each other and found safety there. The youngest child had now grown to become a cute baby. He smiled at us, delivering small noises when he was full and satisfied.

Nasrin told me that she had seen her mother cry every night since I disappeared. Even the stepmother herself told me that she felt lonely and left out when I was out of town. I comforted them that now we would have a better everyday life together in our new house.

It had been a month in Shno when my uncle from Khaneh and his family came to visit. They had lots of food, fruit and even some bath and laundry accessories with them. They gave the toddlers various little gifts to make them happy. It was so much fun that they would stay a few days with us. I loved my uncle and his whole family, but especially his daughter who was three years older than me. After we had eaten supper, Uncle wanted me to go with him to my uncle's. On the way there, he left me a letter telling me that he would come and pick me up in a few days so that Surreya and I could meet outside the city.

As soon as we got in with Uncle, I went into the bathroom to read the letter.

Welcome to Shno, we have many loyal party friends in Shno who take on assignments. We want you to trust one of them who will contact you in a few days. You're going to work together. His name is Shahab, and our code is that he says "package20".
PDK.

I read the letter three times to memorize each word before tearing it into small pieces and tossing them into the toilet hole and pouring on water until I saw them disappear.

We were at Uncle's house for an hour where the men talked and drank tea in one room and the rest of us sat in the kitchen drinking our tea.

On my way to our house, I asked my uncle who had handed him the letter. If it was from a reliable source?

"Yes, it is from a reliable source. I know Shahab and you can trust him. He is wise and experienced and knows what he is doing.

"Next week on Wednesday I'll come by and say I want you to come with me to buy some clothes for your siblings. Then I'll leave you and Surreya in a place where you can meet for a while, while I go and buy clothes for the kids. Write down their sizes and what they need on a note."

"Thank you, Uncle, for being so kind and supportive of me and all of us."

"You're a wise girl and I'm proud of you. I do everything to make you happy. We have the same political ambition as well."

Since we moved to our own accommodation, my siblings had become happier. Now that Uncle's family was with us, the house was full of play, running, and happy laughter.

Uncle's daughter and I sat up for a long time in the evenings when the others had gone to bed. She told me she was getting married soon. The guy she was in love with had sent his father to their house to ask for her hand and Uncle had said yes! How glad I was that she would be allowed to marry her love! But it wasn't certain I could attend her wedding.

***

For three days now I had seen a young handsome fellow with a beard, who every afternoon between five and six o'clock, was walking in front of our house and looking in towards our yard. I became curious and wanted to know who he was and what he wanted. I went out and pretended to throw garbage in the big garbage container that stood on our street. I looked at him and showed that I was curious about him. He followed me to the container and threw a small plastic bag into it and said:

"It's for you. I'm Shahab. We're going to exchange letters here once a week on Thursdays at five o'clock. We don't have to talk to each other. Throw the letter in a plastic bag in the container."

He disappeared in a flash. I tossed my garbage bag and discreetly picked up his little bag. I went to the outhouse right away and read:

I am your contact. We need to put flyers to all households in a discreet and careful way. How many can you take responsibility for? Put your answer with a number in a bag in the container tomorrow at five past five. I'm guarding from afar. Throw it away and walk away. I'll leave the number of flyers you want in a larger bag on Thursday at twelve o'clock in the same container.

As usual, I tore the letter to pieces after reading it twice and tossed it into the toilet hole and poured water on.

I was both happy and a little scared. Happy to have made contact with the party and got a contact man here in Shno. But afraid of being exposed. I didn't know many people here in town, but I wrote that I could take ten flyers to share. That same evening, I figured out to which homes I would hand out the flyers.

***

It was Wednesday morning, and I was waiting for my uncle to

show up. The shopping list for the kids was in my pocket and I hurried to finish all the housework before he arrived.

At two o'clock he came in and everyone was delighted. He asked me to accompany him to the bazaar to buy clothes for the children and I accompanied him to the car. He drove outside the city to an orchard.

There Surreya sat waiting for me, bringing me a thermos of tea and some cookies. We hugged like we hadn't seen each other in years. Then we set the table under a tree. We pretended that we, like the others around us, sat and had tea. Uncle drove off to the bazaar.

"How are you, Surreya?"

"Yes, I feel like I deserve more. No, I feel bad and haven't had any more contact with my brothers-in-law. Reza doesn't keep what he promised my father-in-law. We haven't been allowed to visit Sirwan for a whole month. Since he doesn't have an interest in me any more, he doesn't answer when my father-in-law calls. I'm so worried about Sirwan. But I met Mahnaz three days ago. She is also very stressed and feels that every minute of Khalkhali's arrest is approaching death. She has asked me to find a poison that she can put in the food of Khalkhali and the lady of the house. I've been looking, but can't find anything that doesn't smell, taste, or change the color of the food if she were to mix in the poison. We have said that I would try to find it for her next visit to Mahabad."

"How does her mother act when she sees that her daughter is not feeling well?"

"She doesn't care about her. She thinks only of her husband and hopes to get him out of prison. She has asked Mahnaz why she is not pregnant? It is good if you give birth to a child to Ayatollah Khalkhali, then he may free your father from prison.

Mahnaz hates her mother and does not trust her. But she loves her aunt and comes to Mahabad to see her aunt and siblings."

"But what would happen if you were exposed? Aren't you afraid? Isn't Mahnaz afraid?"

"No, we would rather die than continue life as sex slaves. I'm not sure that Reza, with the help of Khalkhali, really influences my husband's verdict being changed. He wanted to get rid of us and then he'll make sure Sirwan gets executed."

"But there is a chance that both Sirwan and Mahnaz's father can make it and come out one day. You know that various political opponents are trying to kill Khalkhali."

"No, I don't think that's going to happen. Khalkhali has so many idiots like Reza around him. No one can access him. We are the ones who will go under, my friend. I won't be able to see my in-laws sitting around grieving after Sirwan's death. I have to do what I can do before it happens."

"But how? Are you an active supporter of Komala? Do you have any cooperation or contact with the peshmerga?"

"No, no more than that I have correspondence with Sirwan's brothers who are peshmerga at Komala. But if Sirwan gets out of prison, we will join Komala. We've promised each other that. Do you have any connection to peshmerga?"

"I try to help with certain things when I get the opportunity. But it's not easy."

"Are you a Democrat or Komala?"

"I like both, but for the respect of my father, I'm a Democrat supporter."

"I understand that. I like all peshmerga no matter which party they belong to. They sacrifice their lives for our freedom."

"But Surreya, how could we keep in touch a little better? What if you end up in a difficult position and need help? I want to be there for you if you need me."

"Your uncle is our best bond. He has also promised to help me and help us stay in touch. We don't have a better solution right now. You also need to be careful about what you do. I don't want to hear that you've also ended up in danger or jail."

After an hour, Uncle came back. He sat and had tea with us before it was time to drive back home. It was a nice meeting, but it also gave me a lot to think about and be concerned about.

***

It was Thursday and at five o'clock I was picking up my share of the flyers from the dumpster. I walked a little nervously and looked out the door to see if Shahab would show up before five. At ten to five he came walking towards our street. I hid halfway behind the front door. He saw me. We looked at each other and confirmed with glances that it was okay. He walked past the container, quickly looked around and tossed in his bag. Then he disappeared from there just as quickly. With two filled garbage bags, I approached the container. My hands shook a little and the palpitations burst in my chest as I tossed the garbage and discreetly picked up his bag. I hid it under my chador and quickly went back home. I had already fixed a hiding place for the stack of flyers, made a hole in the roof of the outhouse, and put several plastic bags to put the flyers in. The hole was covered with a plastic briquette of the same shape and color as the others.

Before nightfall, my stepmother wanted me to go and get some things my aunt had given us. Aunt lived three blocks from us. Nasrin, my sister wanted to come along. We wore chador which is all-over thick fabric. Nasrin was thirteen, very sweet but childish. It was possible to deceive her with candy or money. The flyers were in my purse under my chador. We walked through all of the city's business streets. Nasrin got some tuman so she could go to the pastry shop and buy some bamia, sweet little deep-fried cookies, which she loved. I would wait for her outside our aunt's house, we decided. As soon as Nasrin disappeared, I went into the narrow alley and put a flyer in the gap under each door. I quickly left the narrow street towards the main square and walked briskly towards my aunt's street. Nasrin wasn't there yet. A few leaflets remained to be handed out, so I took the opportunity to leave them at some doors in my aunt's neighborhood. Outside my aunt's door, I was waiting for my sister. A pasdar's car appeared. I pretended not to see it. But it stayed in front of me. A pasdar stepped out and asked.

"Why are you standing here? Who are you waiting for?"

"I'm waiting for my little sister and we're going home to my aunt here."

"Where's your little sister?"

"She's buying some bamia and there she comes."

He looked at her until she arrived. I saw that Nasrin was frightened.

He wanted her to show him what she had in the bag. She took out a bamia. He looked at us a little mysteriously again and went his way.

I was a little scared that they might have followed me. Had they seen what I'd done?

We went into the aunt who was sitting out in the yard cooking. She was very happy to see us. My aunt was a sad mother who had lost her youngest son in our struggle for freedom. He was only twenty-three years old and newly married when the regime took over Shno. He followed his uncle's (my father's) party and became a peshmerga. Barely six months later, he was killed in a battle between peshmerga and regime forces in the area. My aunt also mourned my father, who was her youngest brother, in prison. She quickly put the things she had donated to us in two plastic sacks as well as a lunch box with the food she had cooked. She followed us all the way to our street to help carry and so we wouldn't be scared now that it was starting to get dark.

After her son's death, my aunt had continued to have contact with his party and fellow peshmerga. She often baked lots of bread, prepared various dishes, bought hygiene items and went off to the peshmerga in the mountain area. She could stay a whole month sometimes. But so far, the regime hadn't messed it up for her. We had occasionally talked about my interest in participation in the party's secret work in the city. But she thought I was needed more at home for my siblings and my family. Better not to put myself in danger. But I knew that if I or Surreya needed her help, she wouldn't say no.

Her fallen son's wife still lived at her house. She was from the Eshireta Shikak, an ancient Kurdish clan found in both the Iranian and Iraqi parts of Kurdistan. According to her clan culture, she had to wait three years after her husband's death before she could remarry. She had chosen to stay with her in-laws for the three years. My aunt and her husband loved her as their own daughter and enjoyed her greatly.

After we had eaten our supper and cleaned up the kitchen, I wanted to sit in the other room to sew because I had received a lot of orders here in Shno as well. Stepmother wanted to talk to me alone!

We went out into the yard and sat down.

"Shemal, I'm so grateful that my kids have you as their big sister. I am grateful for myself that you relieve me so much. But I'm a little worried about some behaviors you have. You do certain things and I know you're politically engaged. But have you considered that we won't be able to do without you? Do you know that your father in prison can die of grief if something happens to you? Shoresh will also die of grief."

"But, bajeh, what have I done? What behavior are you talking about?"

"I know you had to go underground because you had contact with some dangerous people who are politically active. Isn't it enough that your father is in prison for that?"

"I don't have contact with any dangerous people. I don't know what you're talking about. You see what I do twenty-four-seven at home. How can I get in touch with other people?"

"Okay, I'm just afraid of losing you. You are such an important support for your younger siblings, and I want you not to put yourself in danger for their sake."

I hugged her and promised I would be careful.

We had received an invitation to Uncle's daughter's wedding in Khaneh two weeks later. As a wedding gift, I wanted to sew bedding and embroider a bedspread. Uncle and daughter would come to me for the choice of fabric, embroidery model, thread, etc. I was hoping my uncle would bring letters from Surreya with him then.

***

A few days later, all the cousins would go home to our old aunt and help with a big cleaning. It was a tradition that we young people gathered with her once or twice a year and cleaned and washed the whole house. Then she baked good bread over a tandoor, a cylinder-shaped clay oven fired with wood or charcoal, and grilled meat or chicken over the fire afterwards. It became like a party.

We hung out, talked and laughed while we worked. In the courtyard there was a large walnut tree that was said to be a hundred years old. For all the years, the entire family had received several kilograms of walnuts each from that tree. The old tree provided such a pleasant shade on warm sunny days. We always sat outside under the tree and ate when we were at Aunt's home. She had always been the focal point of the family. When she was younger, the family lived with their animals as nomads. They moved to the green mountain area in the spring and stayed all summer anyway until late autumn. We children used to spend part of our school holidays with her in their nomad tents. Being there, close to nature and animals as well as all cousins gathered in one place are the best childhood memories I have.

I was really looking forward to these meetings every time we would clean. The aunt and her husband were now over sixty years old and very sad after losing the youngest son in the war. But when we gathered, we saw that Auntie was happy. She talked and joked with us and even laughed sometimes.

At ten o'clock in the morning we were all gathered under the walnut tree. Aunt had baked good navsilk, deep-fried bread with cheese in it, which we ate as breakfast along with sweet tea. They were so good that you could eat several pieces at once.

I would wash and polish all the windows in the house. We had Kurdish music on a tape recorder. The outside door was locked because music was forbidden to play by the regime. Aunt baked and cooked for us and her still black-clad daughter-in-law helped her.

My cousin Khajij, who was my absolute favorite cousin, finished her task of cleaning the kitchen and came to me to help clean the small windows. She made me laugh so much with her joking and funny way that my tears flowed. In her company, I forgot all my sorrows and difficulties in life.

In just under two hours, the cleaning was done, but we had a lot of bedding, sheets, curtains and rugs to wash after lunch.

We gathered under the tree around a large sofa and each ate a chicken roll, babola, which consisted of freshly baked flatbread, tomato, parsley, cilantro and chicken grilled over the fire. We were given mastav, diluted natural yogurt, to drink.

Aunt heated water in large metal pots over the tandoor.

The younger ones had to get water and detergent for us older cousins who washed everything by hand. We rinsed thoroughly with cold water and hung the laundry to dry.

As a thank you for the help, Aunt handed out a small cloth bag to all of us with something in it, such as some money, candy or jewelry. When she handed me the bag, she whispered in my ear that I would open it when I was alone. There was something secret in it.

***

Once home, I went to the outhouse and found two ten-dozen banknotes and a rolled paper wrapped in a cloth in the bag.

The message read:

There will be an elderly man as a beggar at your house next week. He has some material in a sack that he leaves to you. Hide the material until you receive a letter through your contact Shahab. The beggar calls himself Seid Khalid. PDK.

I read it a few times. I tore the paper into small pieces and threw them into the toilet hole like I used to.

The days went on as usual. Uncle had decided that he would drive us all to Khaneh on Thursday afternoon to attend Uncle's daughter's wedding. I was happy to hear that.

My stepmother and I chatted and ate sunflower seed out in the yard with the outdoor door open. A man with a green turban on his head and a sack on his back came in a little limping.

He asked for minimum contributions for survival. He was old and disabled, he said. I asked what his name was.

"Seid Khalid!"

My stepmother went in to get her wallet to give him a grant. I took the opportunity to show the man, who I understood to be the messenger, the outhouse and said that he could leave the package there against the roof. He understood, confirmed, and nodded.

He was given three tuman and a roll of bread with cheese in it. He thanked and asked if he could borrow the toilet. Stepmother showed him to the outhouse. When, after a while, he came out, I followed him to close the gate. He whispered that the package was too big to be penetrated into the hole in the ceiling, so he left it in the toilet bin.

I went straight to the outhouse and hid the bag which was quite heavy under the brick slab.

***

There were only a couple of days left until the wedding. We were busy with the preparations. But I had an uneasy gut feeling that something unpleasant was going to happen. I had to leave the hidden things to Shahab before we would drive to Khaneh. Often, I looked out to the street for him, but he did not appear. My aunt should be able to help me because she left me the letter. I went back to my aunt's house. She sat, as usual, in the shade under the tree.

"Hey, Pleh, how are you?"

"Good, my daughter, what's happened? I see concern in your eyes."

"Pleh, who gave you the letter you put in my bag?"

"Someone from the peshmerga side. They come here sometimes, and I do everything for them. I know you're working for them. You can trust me."

"Pleh, I got a heavy package from the messenger the other day. The letter says Shahab would pick it up next week. We are going to Khaneh this Thursday evening. I dare not keep the package with us when we are out of town."

"I'll see Shahab tonight; I'll talk to him then. He may come tomorrow at ten o'clock and fetch it. You get to monitor the time and when you see him on the street, you leave the package in the container without talking to him."

"How nice, thanks, Pleh. Who is Shahab?"

"He's a great guy, they're three brothers, they're all sympathizers of PDKI and support the peshmerga. Shahab was my fallen son's childhood friend. He visits me often. I love him and trust him like my own son."

The next day, ten to ten o'clock, I saw Shahab walking along our street. I grabbed my two garbage bags and the bag he was supposed to have and headed for the container. He was standing in a corner behind a house, looking at me from afar. I threw away the two large bags and discreetly showed him the third bag and carefully put it in the container and walked away. Just before I walked in, I looked back and saw Shahab leave the container with the bag in his hand. It felt like a heavy burden had been lifted from my shoulders.

It was Thursday and we had packed our bags for the trip to Khaneh. The whole family had gathered at Uncle's house. It was the night before the wedding and then they celebrated henna night at the bride's. All the young people of the family and the bride's closest friends gathered with her. We ate, drank, danced and painted our palms with henna.

There were about fifty of us in the house. Most of them were relatives of the bride. The older adults slept at the home of relatives while the younger ones stayed with the bride. It was eleven o'clock in the evening. Most of the adults had left us and we were fifteen young girls who remained with the bride. Some sat and painted their nails; others dyed their hair. The wedding dress was tried on for tomorrow. I couldn't help but call Surreya and sneaked into the room where the phone was.

"Hey, who is it?"

"Hi, Surreya, It's me. Hope I didn't wake you up."

"Hi, Shemal gyan, no worries. Where are you?"

"At my uncle's, it's his daughter's wedding tomorrow. We're all here. Can I see you tomorrow?"

"Yes, I'm also invited to the wedding. See you for sure then, when the bride and groom arrive at the wedding venue. We can take the opportunity to find a place where we can talk alone. I'm coming along with my sister-in-law. But we have to be discreet."

"Okay, fine. See you tomorrow. Good night, friend."

I snuck out of the room to the hall again. No one had noticed. We were awake anyway until midnight. Then everyone slept on the floor here and there in the house. I slept with my cousin, the bride. She needed to talk, she said.

We lay next to each other on a mattress. She began to cry.

"What is it? Why are you crying?"

"I'm going to miss my mom and my family and you. It's going to be tough for a while to get into a new family."

"Yes, but you and your husband love each other, you have

your own room, it'll be fine."

"You know I have a secret to tell you."

"What secret? I'm listening."

"We're going to leave the city in a couple of weeks. We're going to join Komala and become peshmerga."

"Huh.... Why?"

"My husband has been a supporter since the peshmerga left the city. He wants to go there. He was just waiting to have me along. I will leave my family and therefore I am sorry. But I love him and go with him anyway."

"My dear cousin, I will miss you too."

"But I know you'll be there soon, too. I know that!"

"Yes... I don't know. I have a great responsibility on me, for my siblings and can't leave them alone."

"But what about that guy you were in love with?"

"He's gone! I don't know where he is. But I have so much else to think about that I've forgotten about him."

We fell asleep at dawn and woke up in the morning to someone shouting, "Breakfast for the ones who are hungry."

Then we helped the bride with a high-end wedding hairstyle, party makeup, and finally her Kurdish wedding dress. She became very beautiful! We also got ready and put on our Kurdish party clothes.

***

At four o'clock in the afternoon, the groom came in his own car, decorated with flowers, to pick up his bride. We followed in different cars to the large party room a bit outside the city.

The Islamic regime had banned music and dancing and, above all, men and women dancing together. But here many young men and women walked with their colorful Kurdish clothes and without a shawl on their hair. They danced Kurdish folk dances, hand in hand, in a ring-shaped group dance. The groom's father was a rich man and had certainly bribed the regime's officers so that they would not come by the premises for control. Outside, a dozen young men stood as guards on behalf of the groom's father. It was a very nice party. The bride and groom were placed in the high seat of the flower-adorned room. There were certainly over three hundred guests. Tea, soda and cookies were served to everyone. Cheerful Kurdish music played by a live orchestra echoed throughout the hall. Some danced and some stood watching. I was looking for Surreya. Right at the entrance, she stood with a few other women. I took a tray of tea and walked up to them, pretending to be serving tea to the guests. She saw me and understood the game. They each took a teacup. I left them and headed the other way. Surreya came behind me and said:

"Go to the right where the closets are!"

We crowded behind the closets, and she started talking.

"I've found what Mahnaz wants from me. I'm waiting for her aunt to call. Then I go to Mahabad and meet her and leave the poison to her."

"Ugh! I begin to feel the danger, Surreya. Please be careful! Be responsive if something happens to Mahnaz so you can hide or join your brothers-in-law."

"I'm not leaving Sirwan alone. As long as he lives, I live! I'll send letters through your uncle. He has promised to give me a ride to and from Mahabad when I need to go."

"Okay, I'll think of you. You, by the way, does anyone more than my uncle know that we are friends? Have you saved anything with my name on it?"

"No, nobody knows anything. I don't usually save letters but burn them directly. My mother-in-law knows you, but she doesn't know what we're talking about."

"Okay then I'll wait to hear from you soon. Hope everything goes well."

"Yes, we're heard. Fingers crossed. We pretend we don't know each other here at the party. Goodbye, gyan."

She went back to the party first and I a moment later.

I had no desire to dance at the party as I carried so much worry and thoughts and had difficulty relaxing. Behind the bride and groom, I sat on a chair and watched all the happy people dancing. Surreya stood at the door and talked to some. She didn't dance either and I understood why. We were certainly many young girls and boys from whom the regime had taken all joy away. Most of us either had someone we loved who was in prison, was a peshmerga, or had been executed. There was no Kurdish family that had not suffered grief because of the Islamic regime. My cousin, bride and happily newlywed, grieved that she would soon not be able to see her family because they were about to leave the city and join the peshmerga. What a life forced upon us!

***

Back in Shno, I tried to occupy myself with my usual chores. Sometimes I met my cousins and some friends here in the city.

Shahab, my party contact, hadn't called back for a while. The regime planned for the first elections in the area. There were posters and election propaganda everywhere. After the occupation of all Kurdish cities, there had been no election. Now, however, in three weeks, the Islamic regime was to hold its first election and they forced people to vote yes to the regime and Khomeini's rule. They handed out personal election cards to each household and required showing the shenasnameh that was stamped when one had been and put one's election card in the boxes. Thankfully, I was under the age of eighteen and didn't have to vote.

My aunt showed up with us late in the afternoon and wanted to sleep over. She used to do that sometimes and it was so nice. She had cooked kofta, large meatballs in sauce, and brought us a full stew. We had a good dinner together. She told my siblings fairy tales until they fell asleep. Stepmother fell asleep before the children with her baby. I was so reminded of my grandmother when my aunt slept with me in my room.

I fixed a small fruit plate and took it to the sewing room. We closed the door so the others wouldn't hear us.

"Shahab had to go underground," said my aunt, "because someone has been gossiping at pasdar. They are out to arrest him. He said you shouldn't contact anyone or receive anything from anyone but me. I have good contact in various ways with the party and the peshmerga.

"The situation is very sensitive now that there are elections. I want you not to let anyone in your family walk outside the door on Election Day. Some things will happen. It may become dangerous!"

"Will the peshmerga attack the city?"

"Not exactly, but something like that. Better to stay inside."

"Will Shahab come back to the city again? Who will be my contact with the party?"

"No, Shahab isn't coming back. I am your contact, and you should not trust anyone but me."

"But, Pleh gyan, you could be in danger if you get exposed."

"I'm fully aware of that. I can't sit and watch my enemies, who killed my son, rule my city and my people. I don't care if they catch or kill me, feeling like a peshmerga instead of my brother, your father and my son. I must avenge the regime for what they have done to us."

In Aunt's voice strength and determination was heard. Her strength also gave me power.

"Do you promise you'll let me know if there's anything I can do? I, too, want to avenge these heartless mullahs. They are pure Satan."

"Of course, I promise. I feel your sorrow and your strength and am with you and for you as long as I live."

I slept tightly in my aunt's arms. Just like when I was a child and fell asleep with my grandmother, I could smell my grandmother's scent in my aunt's arms. A scent that reminded me of all the love and security my grandmother gave me as a child.

***

It was the first Election Day in all Kurdish parts of Iran. As early as five o'clock in the morning, several speakers had begun with cheerful exclamations that after eight o'clock the polling stations would be open. All were welcomed to leave their voting cards in the ballot boxes. Cakes and juice were offered at all polling stations.

After breakfast, I told my siblings that today I wasn't going to sew or do anything but play with them.

"Should we play school? I will be your teacher and you will be a student. You get lunch and tea at breaks from me. No one is allowed to go out today!"

All five liked the idea. Nasrin wanted to be the orderly of the class, mobsir, which meant that she would keep order in the class. For that, she received a bonus from the teacher. We all agreed.

Since the schools closed, I had often had my siblings sit and read and write with me. Sometimes I'd bribed them with candy, pastries, and even bought things they'd wanted for them to join in.

Our large room that was both a dining room and a bedroom became a classroom. First, we all sang a song and told a funny story. Then we started with dictation, where I read a text and they wrote the text which I then corrected. Stepmother wasn't going to go to the polling station unless Uncle came to pick her up. She promised to fix the children's favorite food for lunch.

At half-past nine o'clock we heard a first explosion and five minutes later an even more powerful one. We heard pasdar cars driving around our street.

They shouted into the speakers that Zedeh Enqelab, in other words the peshmerga, was here and had attacked our polling stations. But they encouraged people to come to the mosque and put their voting cards in the box there.

An hour later, several explosions were heard again that caused our entire house to shake. The speakers still encouraged people to come to the polling stations.

For an hour, the only thing heard was the regime's pasdar cars. The speakers had gone silent.

My siblings were terrified and asked if there was a war between pasdar and peshmerga. I reassured them. We sat tightly, close together in my sewing room which was smaller and provided better protection. We held each other's hands. Shoresh moved, wanting to sit on my lap to hide his head and face against my chest.

Nasrin cried and panicked. My stepmother held the little baby close to her chest.

We sat for a long time listening to what was being heard from outside. Everything seemed to have fallen silent. Only pasdar cars driving around the city were heard.

There were no more explosions until the evening, but then gunfire was heard all over the city. We sought shelter in the basement and brought both food, mattresses and what we needed to spend the whole night there.

There was no election, and all the ballot boxes were blown up. Then the peshmerga must have entered the city and waged war against pasdar and quislings, local Kurds who have become the regime's armed forces and spies for payment.

The day after Election Day, the regime had declared a curfew throughout the city. Anyone who defied the ban risked being shot.

All home phones had been turned off by the regime. We had enough fresh food and dry goods to make it through for a week. Everyone had been through wars and bombings and now this. It was scary, but we had gotten used to it.

On the third day after Election Day, the regime shouted through the speakers that all shops must be opened. Everyone had to come out and live as usual. I went out on our street and saw the occasional people coming and going. I went to my uncle's house to find out how they were doing. When I entered, I saw that my cousin and her mother were crying. Uncle wasn't home.

"What's happened?"

"Of those who died from the explosions, two were relatives of my mother. One of them was a young guy, my cousin told me."

"How horrible! I am sorry for the sadness. But do you know

what happened on Election Day?"

"Yes, all the ballot boxes were blown up one by one. There was no election. In the evening, there were direct battles between pasdar and peshmerga in the city. It is said that two pasdar are killed but no peshmerga is injured, thankfully."

"Hope no one is arrested."

"Pasdar is sure to arrest many. Best to stay home," Uncle's wife said.

"Okay tell Uncle we're fine and don't need anything. Goodbye."

On my way home, I met a neighbor's wife who had seen several peshmerga some evenings earlier.

She was so happy and optimistic, believing that soon they would come back and throw out those animals, the regime forces. I didn't dare to trust her and didn't say anything.

***

A week after Election Day, my uncle arrived. He had bought us both meat, chicken and some fruit. He gathered us and told us that the regime was on the lookout for different people who they believed had been involved in the events of Election Day.

"I don't want you to let anyone in or talk to anyone. I'll come by myself and buy what you need."

I couldn't help but think of Shahab and what he had done. Where was he now?

Our neighbor across from us came in and told us that the previous night, twenty young men were arrested by pasdar. She mentioned a few names and I recognized two of them. Shahab's name was not included.

A few days later, my aunt showed up. She looked to be

worried about something and told me that Shahab's two brothers were under arrest and that Shahab had joined the peshmerga. She was worried that the arrested young people could, under torture, mention the names of other sympathizers of peshmerga and activists. Her eyes met mine and I knew she was worried about me. She wished I would move out and live somewhere else until the situation had calmed down. "But that's not possible," my stepmother and I told her. Concerned, she left us!

At eight o'clock in the evening, a man with a gun who spoke Kurdish and was stressed came to us.

"You have to get out of the city now at once! I've got a list of ten people to be arrested tonight. Your name is at the top of the list. I can't let that happen! Your father has saved me from death once and for many years has supported me and my poor family.

"Therefore, I cannot let you be arrested and executed. I'm one of pasdar's managers now. People call me djash, but I have a conscience. Hurry up and take what you need, I'll drive you, in my pasdars car, out of town. From there, I'll get you where the peshmerga group is!"

My stepmother and I were petrified by shock.

"How am I supposed to know you're telling the truth?"

He showed us the list with my name at the top and orders for arrest from the Supreme Revolutionary Court, Dadgahe Enqelab.

"I need to talk to my uncle," I said.

He yelled and said:

"Don't you understand what I'm saying? Thirty more minutes and it's over for you. I can't save you then."

My stepmother said with tears in her eyes that I should hurry up and go with him.

I quickly changed. Put some clothes in a small bag and

hugged my siblings who stood with tears running down their cheeks, staring at me uncomprehendingly, and terrified. I followed the man to his military car with pasdar's badge on it. He placed me in the back seat, wanting me to cover my face with the black chador I wore.

He said no one would stop the car, but if anyone did, he would say I was his sick wife, and we were on our way to Nagadeh Hospital.

He told me about my father and how he had helped him all these years. He told me a lot about my childhood, when he worked in my dad's appliance store. With that, he wanted to assure me that what he said about his loyalty to my dad was genuine and that he wanted to save me.

I felt paralyzed, thrown out into a rushing river where the waves pulled me in different directions, but was neither angry, scared, nor emotionally charged. And I was absolutely unsure of where I would end up.

***

As we left Khaneh and approached a village a few miles away, he stopped the car. He pointed to small points of light in the darkness.

"Where it shines is Badinawe, which is not controlled by us. The village is under peshmerga and opposition rule. It is impossible to drive closer to the village because then the peshmerga will shoot at the car. But if you go there, they'll see that you're a woman and they'll stop you and interrogate you. Do not be afraid. They don't shoot lonely walking women. Go quickly and don't look around you. It's going to be fine. Hope you are saved now otherwise your death sentence is clear at

Dadgahe Enqelab."

Without saying anything to him, I grabbed my little bag and walked at a rapid pace in the dark towards the tiny shining points far away. My own voice echoed in my ears. "How far do I need to go? Will he shoot me from behind? Is it true that there are peshmerga forces over there?"

I didn't know anything, just went and went. Felt no fatigue, no thirst, but began to feel scared. The closer I got to the lighting, the more scared I became. I heard dogs barking and I became more afraid. I was reminded of when I was only five years old and was bitten by a dog. It was pitch black everywhere and I fell into a deep pit but quickly picked myself up again. The dogs were heard ever closer. I hoped someone soon caught sight of me and called out to me. My steps became slower and slower as I could now clearly see the village and the houses. What would I do now? What door would I dare to knock on? I stood and watched, and some distance away I saw a strange bright lighting. I started talking to myself.

"Maybe it's a guard station, Payga. But does it belong to pasdar or peshmerga? Don't know but what choice do I have? I just have to keep going in that direction."

I continued forward and suddenly heard a male voice.

"Hey stay! Who are you? Where are you going?"

"I need help, I don't know where I'm going."

"Why are you out alone this late at night?"

"I had to run away from home. Please help me."

"Give up your bag. Raise your hands and move forward faster."

I did as he said until he said stop. He pointed with his flashlight towards me. Thankfully, he was wearing peshmerga clothes.

He came closer with his Kalashnikov pointed at me. My tears flowed with relief. He was now standing a few feet away from me.

"I am PDK's peshmerga. Tell us who you are and why you're out alone."

"Do you know Ahmad Kamrani?"

"Yes, why?"

"I'm his oldest daughter. I had to leave Shno because otherwise the regime would have arrested me, along with many more tonight. A djash, who had worked for my father before the revolution, came to our house and showed my arrest warrant. He said several young people will be arrested tonight and I was at the top of that list. He was sure that the regime will execute me."

He came closer and asked if I could tell him more about my father, his position, and party friends.

I answered everything. He asked if I had a secret party code?

"Sure, the code is 2240."

He called through his radio phone. It took a while before he got confirmation that it was the right code.

His voice instantly became friendlier, and he came close, no longer afraid of being ambushed.

"Welcome to freedom, my sister. Do not be afraid. We will take care of you."

He carried my bag, and we went into the village. He knocked on one of the first doors closest to the peshmerga's sentry. An elderly gentleman opened and welcomed us in right away. He recognized the peshmerga. We entered a room where the entire floor was covered in hand-woven rugs. Wool mattresses, duvets and pillows were stacked against a wall and had been covered with an embroidered fabric. An older lady and two younger women got up and met us. The lady came over and kissed me on the forehead and welcomed me. She introduced the two younger women, one as her daughter-in-law and the other as her daughter. My peshmerga friend told the family that I was the daughter of an important person in PDK, who was now in prison.

"Take care of her until tomorrow or the day after tomorrow. Then a peshmerga will arrive and takes her up to base camp."

He left us. The women offered me tea and some food while the older couple talked welcomingly and kindly with me. They told me that both their son and son-in-law were peshmerga. Therefore, the two women lived with them. When I told him whose daughter I was, the elder lord immediately confirmed that he knew my father and had met him a few years earlier.

After dinner, the younger women showed me to the washbasin. I washed my feet, face and hands. Then they showed me I could sleep with them on a mattress in one corner of the room and the older couple in the other corner. Tired and safe, I fell asleep instantly.

Early in the morning I woke up to hear the older lady praying. After a lovely rural breakfast of fresh baked flatbread, homemade yogurt, butter, honey and tea, I offered to help pick up and wash dishes, but the older lady abruptly said no.

"You're our guest and you're not going to work; we can sit together and talk instead."

One more night I was left behind, but was told that early the following morning, I would accompany a group of peshmerga to their base. From the family, I got a pair of peshmerga pants, a sweater and a pair of boots. My female clothes were exchanged for male peshmerga clothes. My stripped clothes were left for the younger women.

***

At eight o'clock in the morning after a steady breakfast, I was ready to accompany the peshmerga group consisting of four men. We walked many kilometers, up mountains and down through deep valleys. After five hours of hiking, we approached a valley between two mountains where the group pointed and showed that these tents were the peshmerga group from Shno. The leader who was responsible for the Shno-group treated me well. He introduced some of the men on the spot and then he took me to one of the tents where there were young girls who were also peshmerga. I got to share tents with them.

After two weeks of a lot of information about all the procedures, the leader informed me that I must attend a training camp. There I would learn how to handle weapons, the rules of war, first aid in war, communication via radio telephone and more. He told me that no one could get weapons or take on missions as a peshmerga before they had completed the training. I was happy and grateful to start my education so soon.

The training camp was far away, right on the border with Iraq. A man was going to Khaneh, and I hurried and asked him to send a letter to my uncle. In the letter I wrote that I was now with the peshmerga, felt good and would be trained to become a peshmerga.

When I came down to the tent with my letter where the messenger was, I saw Shahab there. I was so happy and surprised that I spontaneously hugged him, but immediately noticed that it wasn't done right by me. Some raised their eyebrows and questioned my reaction. But Shahab showed joy at seeing me there. The messenger, who confirmed that he knew my uncle as a friend and supporter of the party, received the letter.

I asked if Shahab was here temporarily or placed. He replied that he was on his way to the training center. Silently, I cheered with joy and asked directly if I could go with him there. It was planned that I would also attend my education there.

The next day, I was ready to join Shahab on the way to the training center. He warned me the night before that we needed to walk at a brisk pace over a hundred kilometers. We each had a backpack, water, bread and a small medicine bag. He had his Kalashnikov, but I didn't have a weapon. The leader on the spot promised to inform me if I received letters from Khaneh or Shno.

During the long road, Shahab told me that in the last bag that I put in the container there was material to blow up all the ballot boxes in Shno.

He never said how or who had placed the bombs in the boxes. Shahab left the city the same night the peshmerga attacked the military and pasdar stations in Shno. Then he joined the peshmerga. He was worried about his eldest brother who was imprisoned. Everyone must be prepared for the worst when choosing to fight for freedom and against the Islamic regime, he said.

He asked if I wanted to be a peshmerga or had to flee.

I answered honestly that I was not prepared to leave my family but had to. He thought that the djash who saved me had done a very good job and must be encouraged by the party to do this for his people.

We took small breaks to eat, drink or pee, but then continued our journey. I felt safe with Shahab and asked if he would like to be my brother. He laughed and replied that he had never had a sister but would like to have a sister now. "But then you have to listen to me and my advice," he continued. I promised to do it and it felt safe for me to have such a brother.

Shahab was twenty-two and asked how old I was.

"Seventeen," I replied.

"There are some risks for young girls joining the peshmerga. But everyone will respect you very much for your father. I will make sure you are not exposed to those risks."

I could only guess what he meant, but we felt we couldn't talk about it any further.

***

We arrived just before it got completely dark. He accompanied me to the principal of the center and introduced me to him. The manager confirmed that he knew me and had been a close friend of my father.

That same evening, I was placed in a tent where four other girls lived. Shahab went to another tent where he had his friends.

The girls had already been here for three months. They had come more than halfway through the training and told us that it had been difficult at first but then it felt better. It was a matter of being confident and not giving up. They shared much of their experience. Everyone was a few years older than me, one of them was twenty-five.

It had been two weeks since I arrived at the training center. I had learned the basics of handling weapons and trained a lot at aiming and shooting correctly. It was an intensive military training. The training leader was an accomplished officer of the Shah before the revolution. He was harsh and demanding, treating men and women just the same.

Shahab was going back to his base camp and wanted to see me before he left.

"How's it going, sister? Have you learned anything?"

"Well, it's moving forward. I will learn like everyone else."

"I'll be back here in two weeks. I'm going past the Shno camp and if there's any letter or message to you, I'll take it with me."

"Thanks that would be great. Take care of yourself and remember that I am waiting for you here."

When you were as busy as we were here at the center, you didn't notice how quickly time passed. It felt like it was yesterday I got here, but that was a whole month ago. Now I knew most of them here and had even gotten my peshmerga backpack and my first weapon. But I had to learn more about wound management, first aid, fire extinguishing and communication routes during ongoing wars.

Baking bread over the fire and on stone slabs as well as cooking over a fire were also part of the training. Here we shared all the tasks such as cooking, baking, washing, etc. No one cooked for us, and no one washed or cleaned for us. Everything was done according to a weekly schedule equal for everyone. A real military school with many discipline exercises.

We slept early in the evenings to get up at five o'clock in the morning.

So far, I had done well and adapted to the routines. Two of the girls had moved to their regular base and two new ones had arrived. We didn't talk about anything but what we had learned during the day. We had some group assignments to discuss in the evenings to report to the training leader the next morning. None of us had been told anything about the other people's backgrounds or private lives before we got here. But the education officer knew everything about everyone. He didn't bring anyone in if this person's home base hadn't provided enough information about his education candidate.

***

When Shahab came back, I was very happy to see him unharmed because I knew he had been off on a dangerous mission. He wanted to take a walk with me when my course time was up for the day.

We walked along a path towards the top of the mountain. He carried a small bag in his hand.

"I was with my group on a mission near Khaneh and we met two of the party's supporters in the city. Guess who I met?"

"My uncle?"

"Yes, I didn't know he was your uncle, but he recognized me. He was talking about you. We decided that he would leave this bag with some things for you in a place along my path. I quickly looked at the content when I got it. But I haven't read the letters that are included."

I got the bag from him and felt like I had to see right away what was in it.

Two letters in envelopes, hygiene items and underwear.

"Thanks, Kak Shahab, how happy I am. What did Uncle say to you?"

"The night you left, pasdar came to your house in Shno looking for materials throughout the house. They yelled at your stepmother and the kids about where they had hidden you. They even came to your uncle and other relatives in the city looking for you.

"Ten youths were arrested by the regime that night. You were at the top of their list. But your uncle said your family is fine now. Everyone appreciates that you are here now instead of in the prison in Orumiyeh. Your uncle said you can send letters to your friend through him. He makes sure she gets them."

"I want to read the letters now. Is that okay?"

"Yes, absolutely. You can sit there under the shade of the tree and read."

I opened the first letter.

My dear friend, now I know that you had to leave your home for good this time. I miss you very much but am glad you were saved. Thanks to the courier Uncle, I can write and send letters through him. Maybe I can come and visit at some point! Missing You, Surreya.

My eyes were full of tears when I saw Surreya's name and handwriting in the letter. She hadn't written anything about her and Mahnaz's situation. But I understood that she was wary and afraid.

I opened the second letter.

My beloved daughter, I am so proud that you are where you are now. You are brave and clever and will be a good peshmerga. Everyone is doing well including your siblings in Shno. Your father has been told, through prison officials, that you have fled. Tell me what you need, and I can send it through our mutual friends. I have good contact with your friend and help her when she needs me. Later on, I'll try to come by and meet you at your base. I'm proud of you, Khala R.

My tears streamed as I read my uncle's letter. His true love appeared in every word he wrote. His entire family, even though I was the stepchild of his sister, had been genuinely loving to me. Even my bonus grandfather had always been more like a real grandfather, both supportive and loving. I had never felt like I wasn't his real granddaughter and was very grateful for these honest, genuine people.

Shahab came back and when he saw that I was crying, he hugged me.

"Hey, sister, you're going to get used to the fact that we're the ones who are supposed to be here. It is our mountains that are our safety and strength and that will protect us. Family and siblings, unfortunately, we have to archive in our thoughts and memories.

"We are peshmerga and we are fighting for freedom. Either we succeed and return proudly to our homes, or we fall and become martyrs in the memory of our people. We have to be strong now."

"Kak Shahab, I have a concern for two young Kurdish women who are severely affected by the regime."

"How, where are they? Tell!"

I told him about Surreya's and Mahnaz's vulnerability and why they had agreed to do what they did. Shahab was very affected. His face grew bright red and full of anger against the regime. He swallowed hard.

"Damn men, who in the name of Islam exploit innocent people! I want to strangle them with my own hands! But how can we help the girls?"

"Sorry, it's not easy. Mahnaz's father and Surreya's husband are detained under death threats. Surreya has written to her two brothers-in-law who are Komala's peshmerga. But as I said, it's not an easy situation. Surreya and Mahnaz have a plan to take revenge on the men. But there is a great risk that they will not succeed."

"I have many close friends among Komala. If I get Surreya's brothers-in-law's name, I'll talk to them, we can work together and make a plan to help these poor vulnerable girls."

"I'm going to ask Surreya what her brother-in-law's name is. But don't talk about it with anyone so far."

"No, no I'm not going to do that. But I share your grief and concern. The motivation to wage war against the regime becomes even greater when I hear how inhumane they are."

We walked back and it felt easier to have shared my grief and worry with Shahab. We agreed that he would bring letters to Uncle and Surreya when he would return to his base a few days later.

Two days later, I asked my group's training leader to get two hours off to write my letters. In the group leader's tent, I wrote:

To Surreya,

Hello, my missing friend, I was happy when I received the letter from you. My thoughts are with you and your friend M all the time. I can try to help to free you from here. So let me know if you think it's okay. Let me know the names of your brothers-in-law. I need to talk to them so we can plan together to help you. I dream of seeing you free from your hell. Hugs, S.

I read it one more time and put it in an envelope.

The letter to Uncle.

My beloved Khala,

I was delighted to receive your letter. My health is good. The things you sent, I really needed. I ask you to continue to help my friend S with everything you can. I'm worried about her. Can you convey my greeting to Dad that I love him and continue his struggle. Tell Bajeh and my siblings that I miss them. I look forward to seeing you soon. Hug, S.

Shahab came by just as I was finishing the letters. He promised to give them to Uncle. We hugged and I couldn't help but remind him that I wanted him to be alive and that we would see each other again soon! He smiled and walked away.

***

I had returned to base camp where I first arrived. My assignment was now administrative. I was responsible for ensuring that the monthly salary of the martyrs reached their families in villages and towns occupied by the regime. Now I was fully equipped with both Kalashnikov and a Colt, as well as a belt with hand grenades and ammunition. When we were on missions in the areas that were under regime forces and djash control, we had to be prepared to defend ourselves and fight if we fell into a trap.

Guard duty at night was now another new task. Three other young women who were also peshmerga lived at the base and we hung out a lot.

The village where I ended up the first evening, after urgently leaving my home, was a few hours' brisk walk from us. A couple of times a month, we women went to the village to wash our clothes and take care of our hygiene with the villagers. They were very hospitable to all the peshmerga. They cooked for us and protected us when needed.

Laila and I were going to the village for bathing and laundry. Just before we got on my way, I was called to the base leader's tent. He was a little sad.

"Hey, did you want to talk to me? Has something happened?"

"Yes, sorry! We have learned that two of your friends in Shno who were arrested on the night you left the city have been executed."

A stream of pain went through my entire body. My throat convulsed and I felt sick. But I tried to collect myself and asked, "Which of them?"

"Omid and Kwestan"

I sat down on a chair so as not to fall. My legs trembled. I cried and saw Omid and Kwestan's bloody bodies in front of me.

"Shemal, we all have to be strong, even you. We are fighting the regime. We need to be able to control emotions."

"Yes, you're right. Sorry, I'm not there yet, but I'm trying."

"I also have happy news for you. Yesterday I talked to Shahab on the phone. He has met your family and has letters to you. The day after tomorrow he will come here."

"Thanks then, I know. Laila and I are going to the village now and we will be back in two hours."

"Great, see you later."

We ended up with the same family who received me the first night. They recognized me right away. The women helped wash us and our clothes in the small washbasin. I tried to hide my sad feelings, but both Laila and the others noticed it on me.

Back at base, I stood guard at night. Perhaps it did me good to think of my friends in solitude in the darkness and silence of the night.

***

When I woke up the next morning at seven o'clock, I heard some people talking outside my tent. When I came out, I saw Shahab standing there with a few more. I walked over and saluted.

"Hey, Kak Shahab, when did you come back?"

"Half an hour ago. Should we have breakfast together?"

We had a common dining room which was a large tent. There we sat on the floor and ate from our usually name-marked plate, mug and cutlery. Then each one washed his dishes and put the things on his shelf or in his tent.

After breakfast, Shahab and I went for a walk. He spoke of the two who had been executed. He used to be their contact person when he remained in the city and he mourned them, but the execution did not come unexpectedly.

Even Shahab's two brothers who were in prison could suffer the same fate. Through the resistance, we wanted to prevent the mullah regime from occupying our area. Fighting and defending ourselves against them was the only thing we could do.

"You, I actually met your uncle again and got these letters. He is a real good and reliable friend of all peshmerga. I hope he doesn't get exposed by the regime."

Shahab left me a plastic bag with two rolled envelopes.

Letter One

My dear friend,

I am so far doing well and will visit my husband and my friend next week via R. I have her requested gift with me. Hope to see you soon. You don't have to contact my brothers-in-law. They have their own concerns! Take care of you and I look forward to hugging you again one beautiful day in freedom. Hugs, S.

Letter Two

Beloved Shemal,

We are all fine. I am sorry for the loss of your friends. Glad you didn't suffer the same fate as them. I'll come by soon and maybe have good news from your friend with me. Do you or your comrades need anything? So let me know before I travel, Khala R.

I felt a tremendous uneasiness now that I knew that Surreya and Mahnaz were about to execute their plan. What if they didn't succeed in it! What if they were exposed. This scenario and these thoughts spun around in my head day and night. I wished I could call and talk to Surreya but knew it wasn't possible.

We received daily reports of new group executions ordered

by Khalkhali. Many young people were murdered by the regime without first receiving a trial and conviction. They punished relatives by forcing them to pay dearly for the bullets they had fired and killed their beloved children or relatives with. Otherwise, they didn't get the body to bury

Our military group leader who was also an experienced former officer planned a major attack on regime forces in the area. This was to remind the regime that the peshmerga existed and that we would not give up the struggle for freedom. He had previously succeeded very well in his strategic plans to carry out attacks against the regime.

We practiced our missions daily. Everyone knew where they would be and what to do at different times, when the attack began on the front lines. We hoped that we would succeed and could take over the control of the area again.

***

It had been a week since the peshmerga attacked regime forces in Shno. Unfortunately, some peshmerga were killed in the battle and we failed to bring their bodies home. They were taken by the djash forces, to show off and scare people. We had received reports that several pasdar and djash had also been killed this night.

The regime calmed down with the imprisonment and executions after this attack.

We were preparing for several similar attacks against the regime in different places in the area. The people of the Kurdish area supported the peshmerga with everything they could.

Shahab hadn't been seen for two weeks. Where could he be? I asked some of his colleagues, but they didn't give a real answer.

Then I turned to the base leader with my question.

"He's on an important mission along with two others. They should have come back two days ago, but we haven't been able to connect with them. It's an intensified situation. Regime forces have spread widely in the area and unfortunately the number of local Kurds spying for them and for djash has increased. They pay large sums of money to get the locals to spy on us."

"I ask that you inform me when you get in touch with Shahab. I'm worried."

"Everyone is worried about them. I'll let you know as soon as I hear something."

Back in my tent, Sonja and I went for a walk together. She wanted to talk to me about something she had said.

Sonja was a young girl who had run away from home to be free from her father and stepmother who were not kind to her. But out of insecurity, she had chosen to marry an older man here. He was at least as old as her father and was previously married and had three children. Sonja confessed to me that she herself had become so insecure and yet more insecure when she ended up here among so many men. She was so beautiful and different that many men would have liked her. Therefore, she chose old Adel, who was kind and protective, as her husband. Sonja wanted to be with me as soon as her husband allowed it.

Later in the afternoon, the base leader wanted us to gather at the food tent. He had something important to inform us about.

A feeling of discomfort came creeping in, so I went there with palpitations. When I entered the tent, I saw the leader and some men standing there full of sorrow. Something serious must have happened!

Everyone stood in silence, waiting for the information. The leader began to speak.

"My friends! We have a great sadness to deal with together. We have lost three of our comrades, who were on an important mission a few days ago. Unfortunately, their bodies have been seized by djash."

It buzzed in my ears and head. I felt a rising wave of nausea through me. He kept talking, but I didn't hear what he was saying. Laila and Sonja standing closest to me saw that I was about to faint. They held me in their arms and discreetly brought me out of the tent. They took me to our tent. The three of us burst into tears. After crying out the worst lump in my throat, I asked Laila and Sonja if they heard Shahab's name.

They fell silent and didn't want to answer right away, looking at each other and hugging me both at the same time, confirming that it was Shahab and his two friends who had fallen in the battle against the djash forces. We cried loudly and couldn't comfort each other when our base leader entered the tent. He sat down in front of me and said with a lump in his throat.

"Shemal, I know you and Shahab were very close, but I promise you that we all mourn the deaths of him and his friends. I promise we won't let their blood dry before we take revenge. We should not lose heart. We must support each other in grief, gather our strength and fight. We should not show weakness. You may cry for a while longer, but I want to see you in an hour with courage, strength and fighting spirit!"

***

A week had passed since we learned of Shahab's death. There had been some military activity going on in various places in the area. The plan was to alarm and occupy the regime and djash forces with small raids and then attack them in a large ambush.

It was day ten after the outbreak of the war. The day before, peshmerga forces had launched a massive attack on regime forces in several ambushs. Several djash had perished. All the peshmerga were furious with the djash group, bought Kurds who fought for the regime for money. We wanted to capture them all and give them a lesson to the effect that you don't turn your back on your people for money.

Three weeks later, the war had subsided. We lost two peshmerga during three days of intense combat. I had been mourning Shahab every day for a while and he was in my thoughts all the time.

Winter was approaching and it was becoming increasingly difficult to pass through the narrow mountain roads. We worked intensively to leave three months' pay to the families of the martyrs before winter came and the snow prevented us.

We were gathered in one of the villages that were under our control. Here we selected some of the villagers who took on the responsibility of handing over money to the martyr families as messengers. Recipients would sign a receipt that they received the payment. A woman from Khaneh was in the village to greet her son who was a peshmerga. When I asked who, I was told that it was Hajar, the bread baker in the city. I immediately sent one of the women in the house to check if it was true and say that I wanted to see her.

She came back after a while and confirmed that it was Hajar, so we went to her. She was very surprised and delighted to see me. We talked for a while, and she told us that two prisoners from Khaneh had been executed in Orumiyeh two days earlier. When I asked about names, she said Sirwan.

"No, which Sirwan? From which family?"

"He who had two brothers who are with Komala. When he

was arrested, he had only been married to his love for three months. His wife stayed with her in-laws, hoping that her husband would be free one day."

The same buzz in my head and the same wave of dizziness and nausea as when I heard about Shahab's death overwhelmed me. I didn't want to believe she was talking about Surreya's husband, but everything she said indicated it was him.

"What happened to his wife? Have you heard anything about it?"

"No, I haven't heard anything about her. She will certainly return to her parental home."

"No, she won't. She will surely come to Komala to become a peshmerga. Then I can meet her and support her in her grief."

I was shaken to think that Surreya and Mahnaz might have been exposed. Could that be the reason her husband and perhaps Mahnaz's father were executed. But what could have happened to the two then? Nightmarish thoughts were spinning in my head. I quickly wrote a letter and asked Hajar to bring it to my uncle.

Hello my dear khala,

I hope you are well. I am in deep sorrow for much that has happened lately. I ask you to urgently send information about my friend S. I heard about her husband and am so worried about her, S.

I rolled the letter like a cigarette and stuffed it into a small piece of cloth that I gave Hajar.

"Please, ask my uncle to answer as soon as possible!"

"Yes, I will. Don't worry. Hearing daily about the dead, fallen and executed is our everyday life and our life in the regime-controlled Kurdish cities. Now we only ask that you peshmerga will cope and bring the whole area back under your rule again."

I left Hajar and went back to our host family to continue with our job there. But I had a hard time being involved, hard to concentrate, to talk to someone or write. I was dizzy and felt sick. My comrades noticed it and suggested that we return to our base.

***

It had been four weeks since I met Hajar and sent letters to my uncle. No answer yet and Surreya was in my thoughts day and night. Nightmares about her and Mahnaz ruined my sleep. I hadn't shared my concerns with anyone here and missed Shahab so much. If he had been alive, I could have shared my grief and worry with him. The days were very heavy and the nights full of nightmares. It had snowed a lot, so all the mountain roads were almost completely blocked by snow. We had ended up in the winter rest period. Many activities could not be carried out during the winter. It was just internal training, discussions, planning, and more.

In Navand, PDKI had both its central government and field hospital with French and German doctors from NGOs in place. Two female companions and I were there for six weeks to learn some practical medical procedures to be able to help the injured and sick in emergency situations. I was very excited about this opportunity. My dream was to become a doctor one day.

Once we arrived in Navand, we were placed in two tents with others. On the very first day, I met many acquaintances from both Shno and Khaneh. We started the next day to follow the German and French doctors and the care team. We communicated in English, and I also had to interpret between them and their patients. I really enjoyed being there and learning important things in healthcare.

When I told one of the French doctors about my dream to

also become a doctor, she hugged me and said:

"Then I hope Kurdistan is a free country so you can work in a regular hospital, not in a field hospital in war."

Time passed quickly and we were soon done with our training in emergency care. We were going back to our base camp. We had learned a great deal; to stop a bleeding, clean and sew wounds, re-lay wounds, connect drips and give pain-relieving syringes. We had each received a backpack with medical accessories that we could use in emergency situations. I felt satisfied and it felt like I had taken a small step towards my goal of becoming a doctor in the future.

We had packed our stuff to get back to our base. There was some driving but for most of it we went on foot. I was both excited and worried, wondering if there was any letter to me with information about Surreya.

***

We arrived late at night at our base. We only had time to meet the comrades who were on guard shifts and then sleep in our tent.

After breakfast, I was called to the base leader's tent. I went in and saw that he had two men unknown to me with him.

"Hey, you called me!"

"Yes, sit here. How was nursing education?"

"Very good, we've learned a lot. We've got our medical backpack too."

"Fine, that was the point."

"These two men are our friends and still live in the city. They have some news and letters for you from your uncle."

"Okay, thanks. Can I get the letters?"

"No, they want to talk to you first."

"About what? I'm listening."

One of the two men greeted me, said his name, and told me that he and my uncle had cooperated all these years with the assignments the party had given them. My uncle had wanted to come by himself to see me, but due to illness in the family could not do so. "He asked me to meet you instead of him!"

"Thank you, what does he want you to inform me about?"

I was so tense and stressed that I became harsh in tone and sounded angry.

"My daughter, hearing about the deaths of loved ones is always heavy. But we have to make it. Your close friend who had her husband in prison has, unfortunately, three weeks after her husband's execution, committed suicide. In the days before the suicide, she left a diary, some pictures and a letter to your uncle to leave for you. Be so good, the letter is unopened, and no one knows what she has written to you."

I didn't feel any buzz in my head and didn't feel bad this time. But I was angry and shaky. I felt like I'd been strangled. I couldn't move my tongue to get a word out of my mouth. I accepted the cloth bag, got up to leave, but my leader wanted me to stay.

The other man got up, hugged me, and introduced himself as an envoy from my uncle. He told me that he and Uncle had met at the prison in Orumiyeh two weeks earlier because he had a brother imprisoned there. His brother and my father shared a cell in the prison. He saw my father behind the glass wall when my uncle talked to him. My father was fine, but he had received an extra year in prison because of my escape to the peshmerga. My uncle said that neither my father nor he was angry with me for what I had done. They were proud. He handed me a wallet with some banknotes in it and said it was from my uncle for supplies.

I thanked the messengers and wanted to get out of the tent, but my leader followed me out while holding one arm of mine.

"I'm not going to leave you alone now. We walk away and sit in one place so you can read the letter. Then I'll be with you in time for support. I won't let you be alone in a situation like this."

"Why? Do you know what's in the letter?"

"No, but I was told that she who wrote the letter has committed suicide. Then I know those are her last words to you. I'm not curious about what's in the letter, but I'm afraid for you and how you'll be affected. So let me be with you."

We walked a good distance away from everyone until we came to a kani, water source, where I wanted to sit and read the letter. I picked up four pictures, one of which was a picture of Surreya and her dear Sirwan when they got married. A picture of Surreya herself with her colorful shawl on her head and well made-up face I understood that it had to be taken before she went to prison to first be sexually abused by the prison guard Reza and then get to see her husband. In two other pictures I saw a beautiful, very young and innocent teenage girl with enormously sad eyes and on the back of the photo it said Mahnaz.

I burst into tears and cried for a long moment on my leader's shoulder before I managed to open the letter from Surreya.

My beloved friend S,

As you read this letter, I hope my soul has been united with my beloved Sirwan's. I have decided not to live on after Sirwan. I can't bear to carry all the guilt and shame within me for letting Reza exploit me and my body to save Sirwan's life. My wise friend, you were right that Mahnaz and I were inexperienced and could be exposed. When I last saw Mahnaz again via Reza, I brought her a small bag of powder. I left it to her during the visit.

I don't know how Khalkhali had found out about our plan or what happened after I left Mahnaz. But a week later, I got a call from Reza telling me that Mahnaz had died in her bed in her sleep. The next day, both Mahnaz's father and Sirwan along with five other Kurdish prisoners were executed. Reza called us at home and informed my father-in-law that Sirwan had been part of a group in the prison that was propagating for Komala and against the Islamic regime. Therefore, he and that whole group received death sentences! Both my in-laws have had severe heart attacks and feel really bad. I don't think they're going to survive. My own family hasn't cared about me. They haven't heard from them. You're not around me. Mahnaz does not exist. My hope of seeing Sirwan again is gone. Why and for whom should I live? I am a disgrace and a victim. Hope you and your peshmerga friends can avenge the regime and the likes of Khalkhali and Reza for what they do to us Kurds. I love you and miss you so much, Surreya.

Afterword

This story tells a true story about some Kurdish women.

In support for my memory, I have taken from my diaries, kept between the years 1980–1982, when I wrote down important events daily.

The grief of having left my family, my country, my friends and everything I have of childhood memories is something that always makes itself felt, as well as that lost loved ones are wounds that often bleed.

Sharing this story alleviates my deep grief over the loss of Surreya, Shahab, Mahnaz and many victims like them.

Unfortunately, the imprisonment, torture and execution of Kurds in Iran continues to this day by the Islamic regime, as intensely and at as fast a pace as in the '80s.

Thanks! – I would like to convey to my husband Per, who with his support and positive enthusiasm has given me the opportunity to complete this book.

I would also like to thank friends Ann for text processing, as well as Curt and Maria who have read, and last but not least, friends Ulf and Lena Sahlstedt for reading and suggestions for improvement.

Thanks also to the publisher Olympia for support and publication.

Some facts and history about the content of the story
The Iranian part of Kurdistan is located in northwestern Iran

in the border area with Iraq and Turkey. The Kurdish population of Iran today is about twelve million in an area of 67,500 square kilometers, which is about one and a half times the size of Denmark.

The majority of Kurds are Sunni Muslims, but there are also Kurds who are Christians, Jews, Yezidis and a smaller group of Shia Muslims.

The language is Kurdish, which belongs to the Indo-European language tribe. The two main dialects are Kurmanji (North Kurdish) which a majority of Kurds in Turkey and Syria speak, and Sorani (South Kurdish) which Kurds in Iran and Iraq speak.

There are several politically active parties in the Iranian part of Kurdistan. The two main parties that have been waging a military resistance struggle against the Islamic regime in Iran since 1981 are:

PDKI, Kurdistan democratic party in Iran. A social democratic movement founded in 1945 in connection with the first Kurdish Republic in Mahabad supported by the Soviet Union.

Komala, left wing of the Kurdish resistance movement, a socialist-communist workers' party. Formed in 1970.

Peshmerga, literally "Those who face death", the national military Kurdish force, fighting for Kurdish freedom.

Some Ayatollahs mentioned in the story: (source Wikipedia)

Khomeini – Iran's supreme political and spiritual leader from the Islamic Revolution of 1979 until his death in 1989.

Khalkhali – chief executive officer after the Iranian revolution. In the international press called "hanging judges" for their summary legal procedures. During his years as chief executioner in Orumiyeh, among others, Khalkhali managed to execute several thousands of Kurds and compatriots. Died in 2003.

Montazeri – Iranian Grand Ayatollah. He was one of the most important leaders after Khomeini during and after the Islamic Revolution of 1979. Died in 2009.

Orumiyeh is a city in northwestern Iran near Lake Urmia. It is a Kurdish town, but there are also some Azeri, who speak a southwestern Turkish language. It is home to one of Iran's largest prisons since 1969.

The Kurds were seen by the Islamic regime as anti-revolutionary, **Zedeh Enqelab**.

People were imprisoned and executed in numerous cases without trial. Many fled to the mountains and joined the peshmerga, Kurdish resistance forces/armed partisans, or the opposition in the border area with Iraq. Thousands of people were murdered by the regime through executions, hangings or under torture. The period has been described as a genocide of its own population.

During the 1979 revolution, the Kurdish parts formed their own democratic government. It became a free zone where all party-political groups had their activities. It was called the autonomous part of Kurdistan. After the Islamic regime managed to take over power, all opposition was forced to flee to the mountainous areas towards Iraq and Turkey. These mountainous areas are still a free zone and neither Iran, Turkey nor the Iraqi regime has any military or political power there.

Some Kurdish expressions that I have used in the text for authenticity.

Bajeh: big sister. You can also call your stepmother bajeh.
Bapire: grandfather
Khala: uncle (your mother's brother)

Pleh: aunt
Mameh: uncle (your father's brother)
Daya: mother
Gyan: dear
Agayeh: Mr.